FULHAM

FOOTBALL CLUB OFFICIAL YEARBOOK 04/05

Editorial
**Patrick Mascall, Tim Beynon, Marc Fiszman,
Johanne Sprigett & Mark Peters**

Design
Daniel Anim-Kwapong, Nick Thornton & Ian Bull

Photography
Action Images

www.fulhamfc.com
Follow the action all the way to the net!

Sidan Press, 22 Seymour Mews, London W1H 6BZ
Tel: 0207 486 7117

Club Directory

Contacts

Chairman: **Mohamed Al Fayed**

Directors: **Stuart Benson, Mark Collins, Ian McLeod**

Chief Executive: **Jim Hone**

Deputy MD: **Lee Hoos**

Finance Director: **Andy Ambler**

Operations Director: **Andy Finch**

Team Manager: **Chris Coleman**

Assistant Manager: **Steve Kean**

Chief Scout: **John Marshall**

Club Doctor: **Chris Bradshaw**

Head Physiotherapist: **Jason Palmer**

Academy Organisational Manager: **John Murtough**

Player Liaison Manager: **Mark Maunders**

Head of Communications: **Sarah Brookes**

Club Editor: **Patrick Mascall**

Director of Corporate Affairs: **Chester Stern**

Head of Commercial: **Andy Oldknow**

Marketing Services Manager: **Emma Taylor**

Commercial Manager: **Olly Dale**

Retail Manager: **Steve Rose**

Ticketing Development Manager: **Harley Evans**

Ticket Office Manager: **Sandra Coles**

Head of Community: **Simon Morgan**

Community Development Manager: **Gary Mulcahey**

Football Development Manager: **Dan Jacquart**

Training Ground Manager: **Kevin Moore**

Safety Officer: **Stuart Farrar**

Ladies Team Manager: **Marieanne Spacey**

Club & Stadium Project Manager: **Nigel Jones**

IT Manager: **Christopher Holder**

Acting Security Manager: **Ian Weller**

Venue & Events Manager: **Simon Allison**

Stadium Manager: **Dave Piggott**

Head of Corporate Grounds: **Frank Boahene**

By Phone

Main Number: **0870 442 1222**

Ticket Line: **0870 442 1234**

Ticket Office Fax: **0207 384 4810**

Clubffc: **0870 442 1221**

Matchday Hospitality: **0208 336 7555**

Fulham Direct: **0870 442 1223**

By Post

Main Office:

**Motspur Park, New Malden,
Surrey KT3 6P**

Ticket Office:

**Craven Cottage, Stevenage Road
Fulham, London SW6 6HH**

By Email

enquiries@fulhamfc.com

Website

www.fulhamfc.com

Ticket Office

Opening hours:

Monday - Friday 9am - 5pm

On matchdays

**9:30am - Half-Time on Saturday and Sunday
Matchday the ticket office will also open
after the game.**

Contents

Managers Message			6

Matches Played

16 Aug	Prem	Middlesbrough (H)	8
23 Aug	Prem	Everton (A)	10
30 Aug	Prem	Tottenham (A)	12

August Monthly Review — 14

14 Sep	Prem	Birmingham (A)	16
20 Sep	Prem	Man City (H)	18
23 Sep	League	Wigan (A)	20
28 Sep	Prem	Blackburn (A)	22

September Monthly Review — 24

4 Oct	Prem	Leicester City (H)	26
18 Oct	Prem	Wolves (H)	28
21 Oct	Prem	Newcastle (H)	30
25 Oct	Prem	Man Utd (A)	32

October Monthly Review — 34

2 Nov	Prem	Liverpool (H)	36
8 Nov	Prem	Charlton (A)	38
24 Nov	Prem	Portsmouth (H)	40
30 Nov	Prem	Arsenal (A)	42

November Monthly Review — 44

6 Dec	Prem	Bolton (H)	46
14 Dec	Prem	Leeds (A)	48
20 Dec	Prem	Chelsea (H)	50
26 Dec	Prem	Southampton (H)	52
28 Dec	Prem	Aston Villa (A)	54

December Monthly Review — 56

4 Jan	FA Cup	Cheltenham (H)	58
7 Jan	Prem	Middles (A)	60
10 Jan	Prem	Everton (H)	62
19 Jan	Prem	Newcastle (A)	64
25 Jan	FA Cup	Everton (A)	66
31 Jan	Prem	Tottenham (H)	68

January Monthly Review — 70

4 Feb	FA Cup	Everton (H)	72
7 Feb	Prem	Southampton (A)	74
11 Feb	Prem	Aston Villa (H)	76
14 Feb	FA Cup	West Ham (H)	78
21 Feb	Prem	Wolves (A)	80
24 Feb	FA Cup	West Ham (A)	82
28 Feb	Prem	Man Utd (H)	84

February Monthly Review — 86

6 Mar	FA Cup	Man Utd (A)	88
13 Mar	Prem	Leeds (H)	90
20 Mar	Prem	Chelsea (A)l	92
27 Mar	Prem	Man City (A)	94

March Monthly Review — 96

3 Apr	Prem	Birmingham (H)	98
10 Apr	Prem	Leicester (A)	100
12 Apr	Prem	Blackburn (H)	102
17 Apr	Prem	Liverpool (A)	104
24 Apr	Prem	Charlton (H)	106

April Monthly Review — 108

1 May	Prem	Portsmouth (A)	110
9 May	Prem	Arsenal (H)	112
15 May	Prem	Bolton (A)	114

End of Season Reviews — 116

Squad Profiles — 124

The Opposition

Arsenal	152
Aston Villa	154
Birmingham	156
Blackburn	158
Bolton	160
Charlton	162
Chelsea	164
Crystal Palace	166
Everton	168
Liverpool	170
Man City	172
Man United	174
Middlesbrough	176
Newcastle	178
Norwich City	180
Portsmouth	182
Southampton	184
Tottenham	186
West Brom	188

Enhanced Fix	**190**
Fixture Grid	**192**

Official Men's Team Sponsor

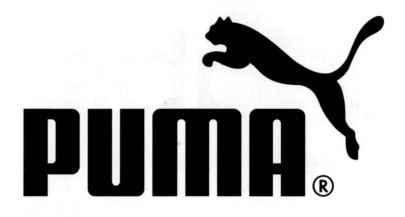

Official Kit Supplier

Chris
Coleman

The 2003/04 season will go down as one of the most memorable in my career in football.

I've always said that being in management is the closest thing you'll ever get to playing and, after a year in the job, that certainly still stands. The thrills and spills, highs and lows of last term were there for all to see, but thankfully we can all look back on a job well done and a record-breaking top flight finish for Fulham Football Club.

Steve Kean and I have always been the first to point to the importance of a collective approach, and that was a key factor in our campaign. The players, the staff and the fans all had their part to play – one no less important than another – and I was delighted to see how the unified spirit and a true "team" mentality paid off. It's one thing having good players, but they're nothing on their own, and I would like to take this opportunity to thank everybody for the part they played.

At the start of the season, the press had us down as firm favourites for the drop but to be honest, that really didn't bother us down at Motspur Park. We always knew what we were capable of achieving. It was just a case of making sure we played to our full potential week-in, week-out. A key part of that was also recognising when it was time to play the slick passing game that people associate with us, and when it was time to dig in and grind out a result. I know sometimes that isn't pretty, but there will always be a time and a place for that kind of attitude. The fantastic away performances at White Hart Lane and Old Trafford obviously stand out as examples of the latter, but the points won were no more important than those we took at Leicester and Birmingham and the like.

The 2004/05 season is going to be just as tough, if not tougher. As I said, last year we were getting written off, but this time around there will be a level of expectation surrounding us. The Premiership is a very

tough league, we all know that, but I'm confident that if we approach our games with the same grit and determination as we did last season there is no reason why we can't push on. We're back at the Cottage which is a huge boost for all of us, and it's also the Club's 125th Anniversary season.

Fulham Football Club is a great place to be at the moment and I intend to keep it that way.

All the best,

Chris Coleman
First Team Manager

Fulham 3
Middlesbrough 2

Chris Coleman began life as permanent boss with a thrilling 3-2 Loftus Road triumph over Middlesbrough.

It was a lively opening in West London, with Boro striker Juninho forcing Edwin van der Sar into action with a volley off Jonathan Greening's cross inside the first 60 seconds.

The visitors grabbed the lead with 10 minutes on the clock.

Carlos Marinelli robbed Martin Djetou before cutting inside from the right and slotting the third goal of his Boro career past the onrushing van der Sar.

But we were level just eight minutes later, courtesy of a Steve Marlet strike.

Jerome Bonnissel crossed from the left, Louis Saha flicked on and Marlet, arriving at pace at the far post, beat Alan Wright to the ball and thundered home.

We almost moved ahead, as Bonnissel's long pass was touched on by Saha to Marlet, whose lob was clawed away by Mark Schwarzer.

Match Details

Premiership
Saturday 16th August 2003
Venue: Loftus Road
Attendance: 14,546
Referee: G.Poll

Premiership Fixture History

Pl: 3 Draws: 0		Wins	⚽	■	■
Fulham	3	6	2	0
Middlesbrough	0	3	4	0

Starting Line-up

van der Sar
Volz — Djetou — Goma — Bonnissel
Inamoto — Legwinski — Clark (c)
Marlet — Malbranque
Saha

Christie
Greening — Marinelli
Doriva — Juninho — Boateng
Wright — Southgate (c) — Riggott — Parnaby
Schwarzer

Hayles, Boa Morte, Knight, Buari, Crossley.

Job, Nemeth, Cooper, Downing, Nash.

Volz and Juninho in action

Inamoto celebrates his goal

10 ⚽ Marinelli (Open Play)

18 ⚽ Marlet (Open Play)

41 ▐ Legwinski (Foul)

42 ▐ Southgate (Foul)

HALF TIME 1-1

55 🔁 Marinelli (Off) Job (On)

56 ⚽ Inamoto (Open Play)

70 ⚽ Saha (Open Play)

71 🔁 Saha (Off) Hayles (On)

73 🔁 Juninho (Off) Nemeth (On)

78 🔁 Boateng (Off) Cooper (On)

81 ⚽ Nemeth (Open Play)

90 🔁 Marlet (Off) Boa Morte (On)

FULL TIME 3-2

Statistics

Fulham			Middlesbrough	
This Season	This Fixture		This Fixture	This Season
9	9	Shots On Target	6	6
8	8	Shots Off Target	4	4
0	0	Hit Woodwork	0	0
2	2	Caught Offside	1	1
7	7	Corners	6	6
19	19	Fouls	15	15
52%	52%	Possession	48%	48%

League Standings

Pos (pos before)	W	D	L	F	A	Pts
3 (-) Fulham	1	0	0	3	2	3
9 (-) Middlesbro	0	0	1	2	3	0

Premiership Milestone

Moritz Volz and Jerome Bonnissel made their Premiership debuts.

Schwarzer saved Steed Malbranque's dipping volley on the stroke of half-time, before Junichi Inamoto missed an open goal early in the second period.

But the Japanese international made immediate amends when he collected from Saha 10 yards out and lashed the ball into the roof of the net for a 2-1 lead on 56 minutes.

Marlet went close to making it 3-1, his studs brushing Malbranque's dangerous ball right in front of goal.

There was drama at the other end in the 61st minute, as Inamoto needlessly handled a loose ball in the area to concede a penalty.

Malcolm Christie stepped up, only to see van der Sar fling himself full-length to his right to make a majestic save.

We extended our advantage in the 70th minute, Malbranque's ball into the box deflecting off Stuart Parnaby's boot for Saha to tap home.

Van der Sar handed Boro a lifeline with nine minutes left.

He raced from his goal line as Doriva's through-ball bounced towards Szilard Nemeth, but he lost the race by some distance and Nemeth lobbed the ball into the net.

Schwarzer made a good save to deny Luis Boa Morte as we pushed for a fourth in injury time.

Everton

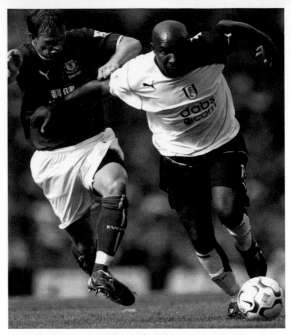

Match Details

Premiership
Saturday 23rd August 2003
Venue: Goodison Park
Attendance: 37,604
Referee: N.S.Barry

Premiership Fixture History

	Pl: 3	Draws: 0	Wins ⚽	■	■
Everton		3	7	5	1
Fulham		0	2	11	0

Starting Line-up

Wright
Pistone Yobo Stubbs (c) Unsworth
Watson Linderoth Pembridge Naysmith
Radzinski Rooney
Saha
Boa Morte Malbranque
Clark (c) Legwinski Inamoto
Bonnissel Goma Djetou Volz
van der Sar

👕 Chadwick, Weir, Li Tie, Osman, Simonsen.

👕 Hayles, Knight, Buari, Sava, Crossley.

Barry Hayles outpaces Everton's Tobias Linderoth

Everton 3
Fulham 1

Three Everton strikes in the opening 45 minutes consigned us to defeat at Goodison Park.

Gary Naysmith, David Unsworth and Steve Watson were all on target, before Barry Hayles pulled a goal back after the break.

Everton boss David Moyes' decision to restore Wayne Rooney to the starting line-up following an ankle injury brought a rich reward in a devastating first half.

Chris Coleman, meanwhile, axed Steve Marlet before kick off after the France striker revealed he wanted to quit the team.

We almost took the lead in the opening minutes when Unsworth's backpass evaded goalkeeper Richard Wright and rolled narrowly wide.

But Everton were soon into their stride, moving ahead in the seventh minute when Naysmith fired home from 20 yards after Watson had fed Rooney.

The home side doubled their lead 13 minutes later. The move began with Naysmith flicking Rooney's long ball to Watson and ended with Unsworth lashing a low drive past Edwin van der Sar.

Everton were clearly in the mood now and from a well-worked free kick 25 yards out, Alan Stubbs' rising drive hit the top of the post before bouncing to safety.

Jerome Bonnissel and Steve Watson go head to head

7 ⊙	Naysmith (Open Play)
20 ⊙	Unsworth (Open Play)
35 ⊙	Watson (Indirect Free Kick)

HALF TIME 3-0

46 ⇄ Legwinski (Off) Hayles (On)

48 ▮ Hayles (Foul)

49 ▮ Pistone (Foul)

56 ⇄ Djetou (Off) Knight (On)

60 ▮ Volz (Foul)

62 ⇄ Inamoto (Off) Buari (On)

69 ⊙ Hayles (Corner)

74 ⇄ Rooney (Off) Chadwick (On)

83 ▮ Malbranque (Foul)

87 ▮ Watson (Foul)

90 ▮ Goma (Foul)

FULL TIME 3-1

The Toffees effectively wrapped it up with their third goal 10 minutes before the interval.

Naysmith headed down a free kick to Rooney, who crossed for the onrushing Watson to head home from just two yards out.

Coleman made an inevitable change at the break, replacing Sylvain Legwinski with striker Barry Hayles.

We were finally starting to challenge Wright, who saved at full stretch from Steed Malbranque before turning away Malik Buari's header.

The Everton keeper had to save twice more from Malbranque and Hayles before we finally grabbed a goal.

It came on 69 minutes, Hayles turning in the box to fire home Malbranque's right-wing corner.

Rooney, who had earlier missed a great chance when clean through, was clearly tiring due to a lack of match fitness and was replaced by Nick Chadwick after 74 minutes.

But by then the hard work had been done, as Everton secured their first points of the season.

**"We've got to realise that we can't go away and play like we do at home - it's one thing saying it, but another putting it into practice. Even in the first half we made some chances and played some good football, but on the flip-side of the coin, when we didn't have the ball Everton looked like they were going to score."
Chris Coleman**

Statistics

Everton			**Fulham**
This Season	This Fixture		This Fixture	This Season
11	6	Shots On Target	**8**	**17**
8	3	Shots Off Target	**7**	**15**
1	1	Hit Woodwork	**0**	**0**
3	1	Caught Offside	**2**	**4**
13	4	Corners	**9**	**16**
32	14	Fouls	**13**	**32**
47%	48%	Possession	**52%**	**52%**

League Standings

Pos (pos before)	W	D	L	F	A	Pts
7 (14) Everton	1	0	1	4	3	3
11 (4) Fulham	1	0	1	4	5	3

Match Details

Premiership
Saturday 30th August 2003
Venue: White Hart Lane
Attendance: 33,421
Referee: J.T.Winter

Premiership Fixture History

Pl: 3	Draws:1	Wins ⊙	▦	▪
Tottenham Hotspur 1	5	4	1	
Fulham	1	4	6	1

Starting Line-up

Keller

King   Richards   Gardner
Carr   Taricco

Davies   Redknapp (c)   Ricketts

Postiga   Kanoute

Hayles
Boa Morte   Malbranque

Clark (c) Legwinski Inamoto

Bonnissel   Goma   Knight   Volz

van der Sar

Zamora, Anderton,   Saha, Leacock,
Marney, Burch,   Buari, Sava,
Bunjevcevic.   Crossley.

Barry Hayles and Tottenham's Dean Richards in action

Tottenham Hotspur 0
Fulham 3

Barry Hayles scored twice and set up another as we powered to victory at White Hart Lane.

Spurs had enjoyed a mini-revival after an opening-day defeat at Birmingham, beating Leeds and drawing at Liverpool, but they were jeered from the field after this comprehensive defeat.

Having lost four of the final five games of last season, Glenn Hoddle needed a good start to the current campaign, but Hayles, who scored just once in the whole of last season, kept the pressure on the Spurs boss.

He struck in the 23rd and 67th minutes, and also created a 71st-minute goal for Luis Boa Morte.

This was the first London derby of the Premiership season, but it was as if nothing had changed for Hoddle, whose team failed to beat us at home or away last term.

Spurs, who announced before the game that they had signed midfielder Stephane Dalmat on loan from Inter Milan, never looked like turning that record around in this match.

The first real opportunity for either side came on 16 minutes, as Rohan Ricketts drifted past two defenders and slipped a pass through to Fredi Kanoute, whose shot was blocked by Edwin van der Sar.

The next chance fell our way, Kasey Keller doing well to deny Steed Malbranque.

We then took the lead, as Hayles latched onto a long-range pass from Lee Clark and got away from both Dean Richards and Anthony Gardner before drilling a shot past Keller.

There was still time before the break for good saves at either end, van der Sar grabbing Ledley King's volley and Keller keeping out a chip from Hayles.

Spurs came within a whisker of equalising when Helder Postiga's header struck an upright, but it was all downhill from there for the home side.

With 23 minutes to go, substitute Darren Anderton's pass put Richards in trouble, and Hayles rushed in to take the ball away from the centre-back before firing home from the edge of the penalty area.

Four minutes later, excellent work from Hayles led to a cross which Boa Morte slotted home for number three.

With some Spurs fans already leaving, van der Sar saved well from Ricketts.

There was a chance for Bobby Zamora, but he was unable to get any power behind an awkward close-range prod which bobbled into van der Sar's grasp.

Event Line

23 ⊙	**Hayles (Open Play)**
30 ▮	**Inamoto (Foul)**
35 ▮	**Volz (Foul)**
HALF TIME 0-1	
46 ⮂	King (Off) Zamora (On)
58 ⮂	Davies (Off) Anderton (On)
67 ⊙	**Hayles (Open Play)**
71 ⊙	**Boa Morte (Open Play)**
73 ⮂	**Hayles (Off) Saha (On)**
FULL TIME 0-3	

Statistics

Tottenham			Fulham	
This Season	This Fixture		This Fixture	This Season
16	5	Shots On Target	**5**	22
40	13	Shots Off Target	**4**	19
2	1	Hit Woodwork	**1**	1
7	1	Caught Offside	**1**	5
24	9	Corners	**4**	20
83	16	Fouls	**14**	46
52%	55%	Possession	**45%**	49%

League Standings

Pos (pos before)	W	D	L	F	A	Pts
14 (10) Tottenham	1	1	2	2	5	4
7 (12) Fulham	2	0	1	7	5	6

Louis Saha holds off Dean Richards.

"The players did everything we worked on in the week – and you can't ask for more than that"
Chris Coleman

August Review

Month in Numbers

Games Played: **3**
Games Won: **2**
Games Drawn: **0**
Games Lost: **1**
Goals For: **7**
Goals Against: **5**

Results this Month

Premiership, 16/08/2003
Fulham 3-2 Middlesbro
Premiership, 23/08/2003
Everton 3-1 Fulham
Premiership, 30/08/2003
Tottenham 0-3 Fulham

Premiership Table

Pos		Pl	W	D	L	F	A	Diff	Pts
1	Arsenal	4	4	0	0	10	2	+8	12
2	Man Utd	4	3	0	1	7	2	+5	9
3	Portsmouth	4	2	2	0	7	2	+5	8
4	Man City	4	2	1	1	8	5	+3	7
5	Chelsea	3	2	1	0	6	4	+2	7
6	Birmingham	3	2	1	0	2	0	+2	7
7	**Fulham**	**3**	**2**	**0**	**1**	**7**	**5**	**+2**	**6**
8	Southampton	4	1	3	0	3	2	+1	6
9	Blackburn	4	1	2	1	11	8	+3	5
10	Liverpool	4	1	2	1	4	2	+2	5
11	Charlton	4	1	2	1	6	5	+1	5
12	Leeds	4	1	2	1	6	6	0	5
13	Aston Villa	4	1	1	2	4	5	-1	4
14	Everton	4	1	1	2	6	8	-2	4
15	Tottenham	4	1	1	2	2	5	-3	4
16	Leicester	4	0	2	2	4	7	-3	2
17	Bolton	4	0	2	2	2	10	-8	2
18	Newcastle	3	0	1	2	3	5	-2	1
19	Middlesbro'	4	0	1	3	4	10	-6	1
20	Wolves	4	0	1	3	1	10	-9	1

Premiership Progression

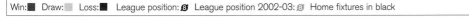

Win:■ Draw:▨ Loss:■   League position: ❽   League position 2002-03: ⑧   Home fixtures in black

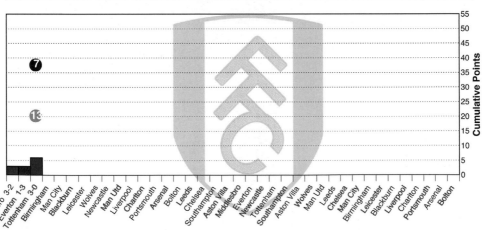

August Review

Premiership Performance

	Aug	03-04
Shots On Target	22	22
Shots Off Target	19	19
Hit Woodwork	1	1
Clean Sheets	1	1
Failed To Score	0	0
Caught Offside	5	5
Corners	20	20
Own Goals For	0	0
Own Goals Against	0	0

Goals Resulting From

	Aug		03-04	
	F	A	F	A
Open Play	6	4	6	4
Set Piece	1	1	1	1

How Goals Scored

	Aug		03-04	
	F	A	F	A
Right Foot	5	2	5	2
Left Foot	2	3	2	3

When Goals Scored

	Aug		03-04	
	F	A	F	A
First Half	2	4	2	4
Second Half	5	1	5	1

Top Goal Scorers

	Aug	03-04
B. Hayles	3	3
J. Inamoto	1	1
S. Marlet	1	1
L. Saha	1	1
L. Boa Morte	1	1

Top Goal Assists

	Aug	03-04
L. Saha	3	3
S. Malbranque	2	2
B. Hayles	1	1
L. Clark	1	1

Player of the Month

Barry Hayles
Goals: **3** Assists: **1**
Despite beginning the season on the sidelines, Barry Hayles forced his way into the first team by the end of the month. A goal from the bench was not enough to secure any points at Everton, but seven days later the experienced striker netted twice, and layed on a third for Luis Boa Morte, in a convincing win at Tottenham. The frontman's display at White Hart Lane was all the more impressive when you consider that he acted as the lone striker in Chris Coleman's favoured 4-5-1 formation.

Premiership
Sunday 14th September 2003
Venue: St Andrews
Attendance: 27,250
Referee: S.W.Dunn

Premiership Fixture History

Pl: 2 Draws: **2**	Wins	⚽	■	■
Birmingham City	0	2	3	1
Fulham	0	2	4	3

Starting Line-up

Maik Taylor
Kenna (c)   Purse   Upson   Clapham
Johnson   Savage   Clemence   Dunn
Forssell   John
Saha
Boa Morte   Malbranque
Clark (c)   Legwinski   Inamoto
Bonnissel   Goma   Knight   Volz
van der Sar

Tebily, Lazaridis,   Pembridge, Sava,
Morrison, Cisse,   Djetou, Melville,
Bennett.   Crossley.

Luis Boa Morte celebrates his goal

Birmingham City 2
Fulham 2

Despite twice taking the lead at St Andrews, we had to settle for a draw against a lively Birmingham side.

Louis Saha put us ahead in the first minute before Mikael Forssell grabbed an equaliser on the stroke of half-time.

Despite being reduced to 10 men when Sylvain Legwinski was sent off for two yellow cards, we moved back into the lead courtesy of a Luis Boa Morte strike.

Forssell then grabbed his second for the Blues, who also ended the game with 10 men following the late dismissal of Darren Purse.

Birmingham came into the game on the back of three clean sheets, but they fell behind to the second-quickest goal of the Premiership season.

Jerome Bonnissel played a ball over the top to Saha, who outsprinted Matthew Upson and went past Maik Taylor before poking into an empty net with the outside of his right boot.

Taylor, on a year-long loan at Birmingham from Fulham, had to be on his guard to prevent his old employers moving 2-0 ahead inside three minutes after a shot from Junichi Inamoto.

Boa Morte whipped in a cross that met the head of Steed Malbranque, but its path to goal was blocked by Upson.

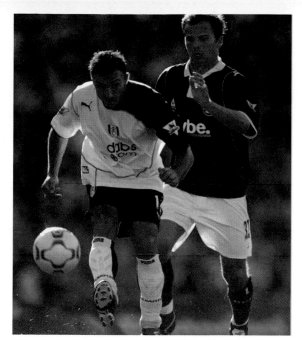

Steed Malbranque gets away from Stephen Clemence

Event Line

EVENT LINE

1 ⚽ **Saha (Open Play)**

8 ▨ **Goma (Foul)**

15 ▨ Johnson (Foul)

24 ▨ **Legwinski (Foul)**

37 ▨ **Inamoto (Foul)**

45 ⚽ Forssell (Open Play)

HALF TIME 1-1

46 ⇄ Kenna (Off) Tebily (On)

60 ▨ **Legwinski (Foul)**

64 ⇄ Clemence (Off) Lazaridis (On)

64 ⇄ **Malbranque (Off) Pembridge (On)**

70 ⇄ John (Off) Morrison (On)

78 ⚽ **Boa Morte (Indirect Free Kick)**

79 ⇄ **Saha (Off) Sava (On)**

80 ▨ Boa Morte (Foul)

82 ⚽ Forssell (Indirect Free Kick)

82 ▨ Purse (Violent Conduct)

90 ⇄ **Inamoto (Off) Djetou (On)**

FULL TIME 2-2

Saha was handed a lone role up front and he proved a handful for a Birmingham defence who made life hard for themselves by continually giving the ball away.

At the other end, Forssell was always Birmingham's most dangerous attacker, twice going close before finding the net in first-half injury time.

Damien Johnson was the provider with a header to the Finn, who chested down before firing past Edwin van der Sar.

Legwinski should have restored the lead in the second half when he met Malbranque's free kick eight yards out, but his shot cannoned back off the bar.

Our hopes of taking all three points weren't helped when Legwinski, who had been cautioned in the first half, was harshly dismissed for a second bookable offence after bringing down David Dunn with half an hour to go.

Things looked a little rosier when Boa Morte found the back of the net with an overhead kick.

But then Forssell equalised for a second time, slotting home after van der Sar had parried Upson's header.

"We didn't get what we wanted, we wanted three points, but we got what we needed, a great battling performance and a point. We also got what we expected, which was a tough game. I'm delighted for my men; they dug in and fought for each other."
Chris Coleman

Statistics

Birmingham			Fulham	
This Season	This Fixture		This Fixture	This Season
18	7	Shots On Target	3	25
26	9	Shots Off Target	4	23
3	1	Hit Woodwork	0	1
12	1	Caught Offside	2	7
21	8	Corners	1	21
77	19	Fouls	21	67
47%	52%	Possession	48%	49%

League Standings

Pos (pos before)	W	D	L	F	A	Pts
8 (8) Birmingham	2	2	0	4	2	8
9 (9) Fulham	2	1	1	9	7	7

Fulham 2
Manchester City 2

Paulo Wanchope's last-minute equaliser secured a dramatic draw for Manchester City at Loftus Road.

City had taken the lead 20 seconds into the second half when Nicolas Anelka's shot deflected in off Zat Knight.

We then equalised through Steed Malbranque, before Louis Saha took advantage of David Seaman's mistake to score our second.

But Wanchope flicked home a late header to secure a point for Kevin Keegan against his former club.

The visitors should have gone ahead from an early corner when Trevor Sinclair's kick found Wanchope unmarked just six yards out, but the Costa Rica striker somehow headed wide.

At the other end, Luis Boa Morte wasted a glorious chance when he hesitated after skipping past Sun Jihai and dragged his shot across the face of goal.

City were resorting to high balls in the direction of Wanchope, who was continually frustrated by the attentions of Knight.

City finally broke the deadlock in the opening minute of the second half, Anelka collecting the ball in midfield and advancing

Match Details

Premiership
Saturday 20th September 2003
Venue: Loftus Road
Attendance: 16,124
Referee: P.Dowd

Premiership Fixture History

	Pl: 2	Draws: 1	Wins ☺	■	■
Fulham		0	2	2	0
Manchester City		1	3	6	0

Starting Line-up

van der Sar

Volz — Knight — Goma — Bonnissel

Inamoto — Legwinski — Clark (c)

Malbranque — Boa Morte

Saha

Wanchope — Anelka

Sinclair — Wright-Phillips

McManaman — Barton

Tiatto — Distin (c) — Sommeil — Sun Jihai

Seaman

Pembridge, Melville, Djetou, Sava, Crossley.

Sibierski, Bosvelt, Fowler, Dunne, Weaver.

Junichi Inamoto challenges Nicolas Anelka

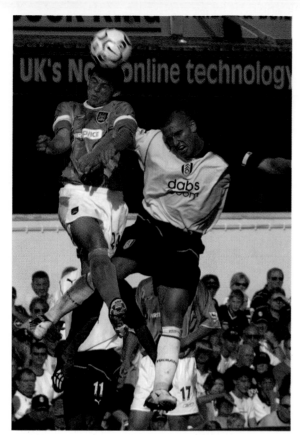

Lee Clark and City's Joey Barton go for a header

Event Line

15 ■	**Clark (Foul)**
25 ■	Wright-Phillips (Foul)
27 ■	Sommeil (Foul)
42 ■	**Inamoto (Foul)**
HALF TIME 0-0	
46 ⚽	Knight (Own Goal)
46 ■	Anelka (Ung Conduct)
55 ■	Jihai (Foul)
56 ■	Barton (Foul)
70 ⇄	Anelka (Off) Sibierski (On)
73 ⚽	**Malbranque (Open Play)**
77 ⇄	Wright-Phillips (Off) Bosvelt (On)
79 ⚽	**Saha (Open Play)**
84 ⇄	**Boa Morte (Off) Pembridge (On)**
85 ⇄	McManaman (Off) Fowler (On)
90 ⚽	Wanchope (Open Play)
FULL TIME 2-2	

on goal before unleashing a 20-yard shot which deflected off Knight on its way into the bottom-right corner. It was Anelka's seventh goal of the season.

Edwin van der Sar made a brilliant stop to deny City a second goal, stretching to push away Shaun Wright-Phillips's long-range strike.

And that provided the foundation for a Fulham fightback, with Malbranque at the heart of the action.

City's defence pushed up in a bid to play Malbranque offside, but the flag stayed down as Moritz Volz found Boa Morte, whose low pass was then turned home by Malbranque.

Seaman was quick off his line to deny Boa Morte, but the former England keeper soon turned from hero to villain.

A comedy of errors in the City defence culminated in Seaman racing out to try and clear a long Malbranque kick upfield. He totally missed the ball, leaving Saha with an easy chance.

But City wouldn't be denied, as Wanchope rose highest to meet a hopeful punt into our penalty area and head home the equaliser in the dying seconds.

Statistics

Fulham			Manchester City	
This Season	This Fixture		This Fixture	This Season
31	6	Shots On Target	4	38
30	7	Shots Off Target	3	36
1	0	Hit Woodwork	1	2
7	0	Caught Offside	3	24
23	2	Corners	4	32
85	18	Fouls	21	84
48%	46%	Possession	54%	50%

League Standings

Pos (pos before)	W	D	L	F	A	Pts
10 (9) Fulham	2	2	1	11	9	8
5(3) Man City	3	2	1	14	8	11

Premiership Milestone

Alain Goma made his 100th Premiership appearance.

Match Details

League Cup Second Round
Tuesday 23rd September 2003
Venue: JJB Stadium
Attendance: 4,874
Referee: A.Kaye

Starting Line-up

Filan

Eaden Jackson (c) Breckin Kennedy

Liddell Dinning Bullard McCulloch

Ellington Horsfield

Sava

Stolcers Buari
Pembridge Legwinski Inamoto

Green Djetou Melville (c) Leacock

Crossley

N.Roberts, Teale, Walsh, Mitchell, Flynn.

Boa Morte, Rehman, Pratley, T.Davis, Beasant.

Martin Djetou in action against Nathan Ellington

Wigan Athletic 1
Fulham 0

First Division leaders Wigan knocked us out of the Carling Cup for the second consecutive season, this time courtesy of a 73rd-minute goal by Nathan Ellington.

Chris Coleman made nine changes to the side that drew with Manchester City, while Wigan were unchanged from their victory over Watford.

Wigan almost took a fifth-minute lead, Peter Kennedy and Ellington combining well to set up Geoff Horsfield, whose first-time drive from the edge of the area flashed just wide.

Six minutes later, the home side showed their attacking poise with a swift, sweeping move involving Kennedy, Horsfield and Jimmy Bullard.

Wigan were playing the better football in the early exchanges, which was perhaps unsurprising given that we were fielding virtually a reserve team line-up. Horsfield again went close after unleashing a right-foot volley which keeper Mark Crossley initially parried before Andy Melville cleared.

Our first chance finally came in the 28th minute when Malik Buari found Facundo Sava, whose header grazed John Filan's right-hand post.

The duo combined again just two minutes later, setting up a free header for Sava which he planted straight at Filan. The keeper fumbled before his defence came to the rescue.

Wigan responded with a curling 20-yarder from Ellington which Crossley tipped round the post.

After the interval, Tony Dinning struck a fine 25-yard shot which Crossley was just able to push round the post after scrambling to his right. Filan then kept things level by turning away an Andrejs Stolcers shot.

Wigan finally broke the deadlock 17 minutes from time, as Ellington rose to meet Andy Liddell's inch-perfect right-wing cross at the far post and loop the ball beyond the grasp of Crossley.

Crossley made his way into the attack for an injury-time corner, but was denied a goal when Filan produced an excellent save.

Event Line

HALF TIME 0-0

57 ⮂ **Inamoto (Off) Rehman (On)**

66 ⮂ **Buari (Off) Boa Morte (On)**

73 ⚽ Ellington (Open Play)

74 ⮂ Horsfield (Off) N.Roberts (On)

83 ⮂ **Stolcers (Off) Pratley (On)**

FULL TIME 1-0

Statistics

Wigan		Fulham
10	Shots On Target	4
7	Shots Off Target	5
0	Hit Woodwork	0
4	Caught Offside	3
12	Corners	7
7	Fouls	14

Sylvain Legwinski takes on Jimmy Bullard

"We got what we deserved – nothing. I decided to give some players a rest, but we still had enough talent out there to have got something from this. It's the first time I've witnessed a lack of effort and togetherness from my team since I took over." Chris Coleman

Blackburn Rovers 0
Fulham 2

Luis Boa Morte in action against Martin Taylor

Match Details

Premiership
Sunday 28th September 2003
Venue: Ewood Park
Attendance: 21,985
Referee: M.D.Messias

Premiership Fixture History

Pl:**3** Draws:**0**	Wins	⚽	■	■
Blackburn Rovers	2	5	6	0
Fulham	**1**	**3**	**6**	**0**

Starting Line-up

Friedel

Babbel   Taylor   Amoruso   Gresko

Emerton   Flitcroft (c)   Ferguson   Thompson

Cole   Jansen

Boa Morte   Saha   Malbranque

Pembridge   Inamoto   Clark (c)

Bonnissel   Goma   Knight   Volz

van der Sar

Johansson, Tugay, Grabbi, Yorke, Kelly.

Leacock, Buari, Melville, Djetou, Crossley.

We continued our impressive start to the Premiership season with a comfortable win over a lacklustre Blackburn.

Goals from Luis Boa Morte and Louis Saha in either half helped us leapfrog Rovers into seventh place.

Blackburn offered little going forward, as they slumped to their third home defeat in four league games.

Andy Cole wasted a good opportunity on three minutes when he shot wildly over after spinning past his marker.

We took the lead on five minutes, Steed Malbranque beating Vratislav Gresko before making his way into the penalty area and crossing for Boa Morte to tap home.

Brett Emerton fired wide after a promising run as the home side tried to respond.

The Australian international then almost conceded a penalty, as Boa Morte went down in the area under his challenge.

Rovers were looking stretched at the back as they struggled to contain the pace of Boa Morte and Saha.

Junichi Inamoto threatened after an angled pass from Boa Morte, but Gresko blocked well.

David Thompson finally provided something for the Rovers

Louis Saha in action against Nils Eric Johansson

Event Line

5 ⚽ **Boa Morte (Open Play)**

25 ◻ **Inamoto (Foul)**

28 ⇄ Babbel (Off) Johansson (On)

45 ◻ **Knight (Foul)**

HALF TIME 0-1

46 ⇄ **Volz (Off) Leacock (On)**

56 ⚽ **Saha (Open Play)**

58 ⇄ Ferguson (Off) Tugay (On)

58 ⇄ Gresko (Off) Grabbi (On)

61 ◻ **Flitcroft (Foul)**

76 ◻ **Leacock (Foul)**

83 ◻ Tugay (Ung Conduct)

83 ◻ **Boa Morte (Ung Conduct)**

84 ⇄ **Boa Morte (Off) Buari (On)**

FULL TIME 0-2

crowd to shout about when he cut in from the left and beat Moritz Volz before blasting wide.

Edwin van der Sar was called into action for virtually the first time early in the second half, but it was a routine save off a Gresko shot.

We gave ourselves some breathing space with a second goal 11 minutes after the break, as Saha outpaced Lorenzo Amoruso before stepping inside and driving powerfully past Brad Friedel.

Rovers boss Graeme Souness immediately threw caution to the wind, going to three up front by bringing on Corrado Grabbi for Gresko and replacing the ineffective Barry Ferguson with Kerimoglu Tugay.

Rovers were looking more threatening and van der Sar did well to tip Emerton's 25-yard drive past the post.

Grabbi and Thompson linked well to slice through the defence, but Matt Jansen couldn't get there to finish.

Emerton then forced a reaction save from van der Sar after strong work by Grabbi down the left.

As the clock ticked down, Cole looped a header into van der Sar's hands before going agonisingly close with a lob which struck the crossbar.

"We came to frustrate them and we did just that. We were very aware that Blackburn have got some great players and I still think they will be a top six side, so this is a great result for us."
Chris Coleman

Statistics

Fulham			Blackburn	
This Season	This Fixture		This Fixture	This Season
39	5	Shots On Target	2	33
43	9	Shots Off Target	3	33
2	1	Hit Woodwork	0	1
29	7	Caught Offside	1	8
37	5	Corners	5	28
111	15	Fouls	14	99
51%	56%	Possession	44%	47%

League Standings

Pos (pos before)	W	D	L	F	A	Pts
11 (9) Blackburn	2	2	3	14	14	8
7 (10) Fulham	3	2	1	13	9	11

Premiership Milestone

Dean Leacock made his Premiership debut.

September Review

Month in Numbers

Games Played: **4**
Games Won: **1**
Games Drawn: **2**
Games Lost: **1**
Goals For: **6**
Goals Against: **5**

Results this Month

Premiership, 14/09/2003
Birmingham 2-2 Fulham
Premiership, 20/09/2003
Fulham 2-2 Man City
League Cup, 23/09/2003
Wigan 1-0 Fulham
Premiership, 28/9/2003
Blackburn 0-2 Fulham

Premiership Table

Pos	(Aug)		Pl	W	D	L	F	A	Diff	Pts
1	(1)	Arsenal	7	5	2	0	14	5	+9	17
2	(5)	Chelsea	6	5	1	0	16	6	+10	16
3	(2)	Man Utd	7	5	1	1	13	3	+10	16
4	(6)	Birmingham	6	4	2	0	8	2	+6	14
5	(4)	Man City	7	3	3	1	14	8	+6	12
6	(8)	Southampton	7	3	3	1	8	4	+4	12
7	**(7)**	**Fulham**	**6**	**3**	**2**	**1**	**13**	**9**	**+4**	**11**
8	(10)	Liverpool	7	3	2	2	11	7	+4	11
9	(3)	Portsmouth	7	2	3	2	9	7	+2	9
10	(14)	Everton	7	2	2	3	12	11	+1	8
11	(9)	Blackburn	7	2	2	3	14	14	0	8
12	(11)	Charlton	7	2	2	3	10	11	-1	8
13	(13)	Aston Villa	7	2	1	4	7	11	-4	7
14	(19)	Middlesbro'	7	2	1	4	6	12	-6	7
15	(17)	Bolton	7	1	4	2	5	11	-6	7
16	(16)	Leicester	7	1	2	4	10	13	-3	5
17	(15)	Tottenham	7	1	2	4	5	12	-7	5
18	(12)	Leeds	7	1	2	4	6	16	-10	5
19	(18)	Newcastle	6	0	3	3	7	10	-3	3
20	(20)	Wolves	7	0	2	5	2	18	-16	2

Premiership Progression

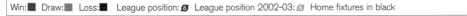

Win:■ Draw:■ Loss:■ League position: 🎱 League position 2002-03: 🎱 Home fixtures in black

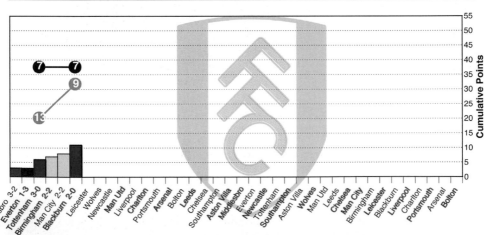

September Review

Premiership Performance

	Sept	03-04
Shots On Target	11	33
Shots Off Target	14	33
Hit Woodwork	0	1
Clean Sheets	1	2
Failed To Score	0	0
Caught Offside	3	8
Corners	8	28
Own Goals For	0	0
Own Goals Against	1	1

Goals Resulting From

	Sept		03-04	
	F	A	F	A
Open Play	5	2	11	6
Set Piece	1	1	2	2

How Goals Scored

	Sept		03-04	
	F	A	F	A
Right Foot	4	1	9	3
Left Foot	2	1	4	4
Header	0	1	0	1

When Goals Scored

	Sept		03-04	
	F	A	F	A
First Half	2	1	4	5
Second Half	4	2	9	3

Top Goal Scorers

	Sept	03-04
L. Saha	3	4
B. Hayles	0	3
L. Boa Morte	2	3
J. Inamoto	0	1
S. Malbranque	1	1
S. Marlet	0	1

Top Goal Assists

	Sept	03-04
S. Malbranque	2	4
L. Saha	0	3
L. Clark	1	2
J. Bonnissel	1	1
J. Inamoto	1	1
B. Hayles	0	1
L. Boa Morte	1	1

Player of the Month

Luis Boa Morte

Goals: **2** Assists: **1**

The Portuguese wide man was at the heart of Fulham's attacking play in September. A spectacular goal in a fiery encounter at Birmingham was followed by an assist against Manchester City. Both these games ended level, but Boa Morte's early strike at Blackburn set the Cottagers on their way to a well-deserved victory. Opponents were unable to cope with the electric pace of the ex-Arsenal man, and he was clearly relishing his involvement in Fulham's stylish brand of football.

Fulham 2
Leicester City 0

Match Details

Premiership
Saturday 4th October 2003
Venue: Loftus Road
Attendance: 14,562
Referee: C.J.Foy

Premiership Fixture History

Pl: **2** Draws:**1**	Wins	⚽	■	■
Fulham	1	2	5	0
Leicester City	0	0	5	0

Starting Line-up

van der Sar

Leacock Knight Goma Bonnissel

Clark (c) Inamoto Pembridge

Malbranque Boa Morte

Saha

Scowcroft Bent

Nalis Izzet (c) Scimeca

Rogers Impey

Taggart Howey Sinclair

Walker

Legwinski, Djetou, Hayles, Melville, Crossley.

Dickov, Ferdinand, Gillespie, Stewart, Coyne.

Luis Boa Morte bagged a brace as we made it an afternoon to forget for former boss Micky Adams.

The Portuguese winger scored either side of the break to take his tally to five goals in five Premiership games.

We could even afford to miss a first half penalty, as we moved up from seventh to fourth in the table.

We came into the game on a high after last week's win at Blackburn.

Leicester, meanwhile, were keen to make amends for their 4-1 thumping against Manchester United last time out.

But neither side looked convincing in the early exchanges and it wasn't until the half-hour mark that the game started to come to life.

Boa Morte was fortunate to avoid punishment after kicking out at Frank Sinclair as the two tussled on the ground following a corner.

And he made the most of his escape, stabbing the ball home from close range on 36 minutes after Steed Malbranque's shot had cannoned back off the woodwork.

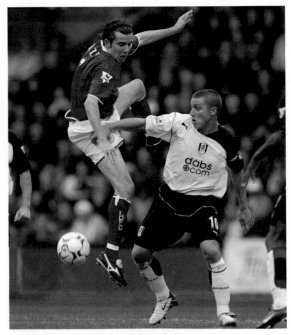

Lee Clark in action against a flying Muzzy Izzet

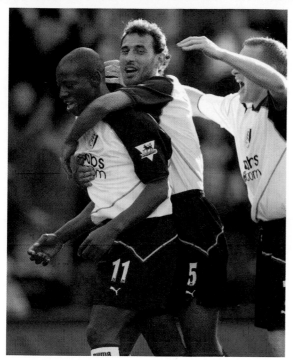

Luis Boa Morte celebrates one of his two goals

Event Line

30 ▪ Knight (Foul)

36 ⊙ Boa Morte (Open Play)

HALF TIME 1-0

61 ⇄ Howey (Off) Dickov (On)

61 ⇄ Nalis (Off) Ferdinand (On)

64 ⇄ **Inamoto (Off) Legwinski (On)**

66 ▪ **Goma (Foul)**

73 ⊙ **Boa Morte (Open Play)**

77 ⇄ Bent (Off) Gillespie (On)

81 ⇄ **Leacock (Off) Djetou (On)**

84 ⇄ **Saha (Off) Hayles (On)**

90 ▪ Impey (Foul)

FULL TIME 2-0

We should have doubled the lead on 40 minutes when referee Chris Foy penalised Gerry Taggart for holding down Louis Saha in the area.

Saha wanted to take the spot-kick himself, but became embroiled in a shoving match with Malbranque.

Malbranque won the argument, but saw his penalty saved by Ian Walker diving to his left.

The visitors went close to equalising six minutes after the interval, as Taggart flicked on a long Alan Rogers throw to Marcus Bent, whose prod bobbled across the face of goal and just beyond the far post.

Edwin van der Sar then seized James Scowcroft's header as Leicester upped the pressure.

Adams decided to throw caution to the wind in an attempt to rescue at least a point, introducing Les Ferdinand and Paul Dickov on 61 minutes to join Bent and Scowcroft in a four-man attack.

But we were now looking the more likely to score, Walker sprawling across his goalmouth to cut out a shot on the turn from Malbranque before Saha headed Malbranque's left-wing corner into the side netting.

It was left to Boa Morte to seal the win with his second strike on 73 minutes, firing home from six yards after his initial shot was blocked by Rogers.

Statistics

	Fulham			Leicester City	
	This Season	This Fixture		This Fixture	This Season
	40	7	Shots On Target	5	35
	41	8	Shots Off Target	3	44
	2	1	Hit Woodwork	1	5
	9	1	Caught Offside	2	17
	32	4	Corners	4	35
	114	15	Fouls	11	127
	48%	54%	Possession	46%	44%

League Standings

Pos (pos before)		W	D	L	F	A	Pts
4 (7)	Fulham	4	2	1	15	9	14
19 (16)	Leicester	1	2	5	10	15	5

Match Details

Premiership
Saturday 18th October 2003
Venue: Loftus Road
Attendance:17,031
Referee: H.M.Webb

Premiership Fixture History

Pl:1 Draws:1	Wins	 ⊙	■	■
Fulham	0	0	2	0
Wolves	0	0	2	0

Starting Line-up

van der Sar

Leacock   Knight   Goma   Bonnissel

Clark (c)   Inamoto   Pembridge
Legwinski   Malbranque
Saha

Blake
Camara   Miller
Rae   Cameron   Gudjonsson

Naylor   Butler (c)   Craddock   Irwin
Oakes

Djetou, Melville, Volz, Hayles, Crossley.

Kachloul, Kennedy, Sturridge, Murray, Ingimarsson.

Barry Hayles is challenged by Paul Butler

Fulham 0
Wolves 0

We failed to score in a Premiership match for the first time this season, as we battled to a goalless draw against Wolves.

We were without the in-form Luis Boa Morte, who had picked up a hamstring strain while playing for Portugal in midweek.

Wolves, buoyed by their first victory of the season against Manchester City in their last outing a fortnight ago, looked threatening in possession.

Henri Camara, revelling in his role on the left side of the Wolves midfield, cut inside brilliantly just before the half-hour and whipped an angled shot beyond the far post.

Our first real chance came in the 32nd minute, Jerome Bonnissel bursting down the left and crossing for Louis Saha to power a header just the wrong side of Michael Oakes' left-hand post.

Saha had another scoring opportunity five minutes before the break, but could only produce an acrobatic slice when attempting to connect with Dean Leacock's cross from the right. Steed Malbranque picked up the pieces and his powerful drive was well parried by Oakes.

Wolves started the second half strongly, Edwin van der Sar pushing away Jody Craddock's brave diving header from Alex

Nathan Blake - under pressure from Legwinski

Event Line

14 ▨	**Leacock (Foul)**
38 ▨	Naylor (Foul)
HALF TIME 0-0	
54 ▨	Miller (Foul)
58 ⇄	Miller (Off) Kennedy (On)
59 ▨	**Inamoto (Ung Conduct)**
65 ⇄	**Inamoto (Off) Hayles (On)**
FULL TIME 0-0	

Statistics

Fulham				Wolves
This Season	This Fixture		This Fixture	This Season
43	3	Shots On Target	6	28
47	6	Shots Off Target	7	57
3	1	Hit Woodwork	0	3
15	6	Caught Offside	6	26
35	3	Corners	8	31
126	12	Fouls	15	134
42%	51%	Possession	49%	42%

League Standings

Pos (pos before)	W	D	L	F	A	Pts
5 (5) Fulham	4	3	1	15	9	15
19 (20) Wolves	1	3	5	3	18	6

Premiership Milestone

75 Sylvain Legwinski made his 75th Premiership appearance.

Rae's right-wing corner.

On 59 minutes we broke into the Wolves penalty area, only for Junichi Inamoto to be booked by referee Howard Webb for taking a dive when tackled by Rae.

Nathan Blake had a chance for Wolves shortly afterwards, but headed over from Paul Butler's nod-back.

We wasted a great chance to break the deadlock when Barry Hayles bundled his way through the heart of the Wolves backline and the ball fell to Malbranque, whose delayed shot was blocked by Oakes.

Van der Sar matched his opposite number two minutes later, sticking out a glove to save Camara's smacked shot on the turn.

Wolves' Senegalese international had a clearer opening 60 seconds later, but blazed over from 10 yards. Butler twice headed over the bar from good positions in the 80th minute. Saha then missed with another off-target header, this time from Bonnissel's excellent cross.

Van der Sar made a superb reaction save to deny Blake's snap-shot, before Malbranque rattled the Wolves bar with a smart volley off Hayles' cross with two minutes to play.

**"We've got to face facts. We haven't got a massive squad full of international players."
Chris Coleman**

Jerome Bonnissel challenges Lee Bowyer

Match Details

Premiership
Tuesday 21st October 2003
Venue: Loftus Road
Attendance: 16,506
Referee: B.Knight

Premiership Fixture History

	Pl: 3 Draws:0	Wins ⚽	■	■
Fulham	2	7	3	0
Newcastle United	1	5	8	1

Starting Line-up

van der Sar

Leacock Knight Goma Bonnissel

Clark (c) Legwinski Pembridge

Buari Malbranque

Saha

Shearer (c) Ameobi

Robert Speed Jenas Bowyer

Bernard Bramble O'Brien Hughes

Given

Djetou, Melville, Inamoto, Hayles, Crossley.

S.Caldwell, Viana, Ambrose, Lua Lua, Harper.

Fulham 2
Newcastle United 3

Sven-Goran Eriksson came to Loftus Road to assess future England stars, but was instead given a flashback to the past as Alan Shearer powered Newcastle to a comeback victory.

We were 2-0 up inside seven minutes, with goals from St James' Park old boys Lee Clark and Louis Saha, but a goal from Laurent Robert and two from Shearer saw United take the points.

In the fifth minute, Aaron Hughes miscontrolled a lofted pass forward down the left wing, chesting it into Steed Malbranque's path.

The Frenchman cut inside and fed Clark, who turned and thundered the ball into the far corner from an acute angle for his first goal of the season.

We doubled our lead just two minutes later when Saha produced an equally smart goal.

Sylvain Legwinski hoisted the ball up to the edge of the area where Saha controlled, burst past Titus Bramble and smacked a shot across Shay Given and inside the post.

It was all action in West London, as Sir Bobby Robson's side pulled one back on the quarter-hour.

Shola Ameobi crossed from the right, Robert and Shearer played a one-two and the Frenchman fired home a half-volley from 10 yards.

Newcastle's increased pressure paid off five minutes into the second half.

Lee Bowyer slipped the ball down the inside-right channel to Ameobi, who raced beyond Alain Goma, only to be sent tumbling by a slide tackle from the ex-Newcastle defender.

Referee Barry Knight pointed to the spot and Shearer sent Edwin van der Sar the wrong way to level at 2-2.

Shearer struck again after 55 minutes to put Newcastle 3-2 up, completing the visitors' comeback.

Jermaine Jenas waltzed into the penalty area, shimmied past Zat Knight and poked the ball towards Shearer, who smacked it into the roof of the net from eight yards.

We had chances to level, with Mark Pembridge snatching at a bouncing ball in the box and Saha drawing a solid save from Given.

Bramble redeemed himself for his earlier blunder by clearing off his own line eight minutes from time.

And Given stuck out a leg to boot away Legwinski's late shot from Junichi Inamoto's cross as United held on to win.

Zat Knight and Shola Ameobi climb for a header

Event Line

5 ⊙	**Clark (Open Play)**
7 ⊙	**Saha (Open Play)**
12 ▮	Speed (Foul)
15 ⊙	Robert (Open Play)
24 ▮	Bowyer (Foul)
HALF TIME 2-1	
46 ⇄	**Buari (Off) Hayles (On)**
50 ⊙	Shearer (Penalty)
54 ▮	**Pembridge (Foul)**
55 ⊙	Shearer (Indirect Free Kick)
65 ▮	**Legwinski (Foul)**
78 ⇄	**Pembridge (Off) Inamoto (On)**
86 ⇄	Robert (Off) Ambrose (On)
FULL TIME 2-3	

Statistics

	Fulham			Newcastle Utd	
	This Season	This Fixture		This Fixture	This Season
	47	4	Shots On Target	8	37
	47	0	Shots Off Target	4	40
	3	0	Hit Woodwork	0	2
	20	5	Caught Offside	5	33
	39	4	Corners	8	60
	140	14	Fouls	16	139
	37%	48%	Possession	52%	41%

League Standings

Pos (pos before)		W	D	L	F	A	Pts
6	(6) Fulham	4	3	2	17	12	15
10	(12) Newcastle	3	3	3	12	12	12

Manchester United 1
Fulham 3

Match Details

Premiership
Saturday 25th October 2003
Venue: Old Trafford
Attendance: 67,727
Referee: M.A.Riley

Premiership Fixture History

	Pl:3	Draws:0	Wins ⚽	■	■
Manchester United	2	7	6	0	
Fulham	**1**	5	4	0	

Starting Line-up

Howard
G.Neville   Ferdinand   Silvestre   O'Shea
Ronaldo   Djemba-Djemba   Butt   Giggs (c)
van Nistelrooy   Forlan

Boa Morte   Saha   Malbranque
Pembridge   Legwinski   Clark (c)
Bonnissel   Goma   Knight   Volz
van der Sar

Fortune, Scholes, Bellion, Fletcher, Carroll.

Inamoto, Djetou, Hayles, Melville, Crossley.

Louis Saha in action.

Steed Malbranque starred in an amazing smash-and-grab raid at Old Trafford.

The Frenchman ran the champions ragged as we stormed to our first win over United for 39 years.

Lee Clark set us on our way with his third-minute strike and United were hugely fortunate to go in level at the break following Diego Forlan's injury-time goal.

But the brilliant Malbranque ran the show in the second half, firing our second in the 66th minute and providing the through-ball for Junichi Inamoto to wrap up a wonderful victory 11 minutes from time.

Malbranque set up the opener with three minutes on the clock when he caught Mikael Silvestre and John O'Shea napping on the right and crossed to give unmarked captain Clark the simplest of chances.

We went agonisingly close to increasing the lead on 18 minutes when Moritz Volz cut the ball back from the right and Mark Pembridge hammered a rising 20-yard effort which clattered the crossbar before bouncing down onto the line and away to safety.

Fulham's Lee Clark celebrates scoring

Event Line

3 ⚽ **Clark (Open Play)**

17 ⬛ Forlan (Foul)

32 🔄 **Pembridge (Off) Inamoto (On)**

42 ⬛ Djemba-Djemba (Ung Conduct)

43 ⬛ **Inamoto (Ung Conduct)**

45 ⚽ Forlan (Open Play)

HALF TIME 1-1

46 🔄 Silvestre (Off) Fortune (On)

50 ⬛ Fortune (Ung Conduct)

58 ⬛ Giggs (Foul)

66 ⚽ **Malbranque (Open Play)**

69 🔄 Ronaldo (Off) Scholes (On)

74 🔄 **Bonnissel (Off) Djetou (On)**

79 ⚽ **Inamoto (Open Play)**

80 🔄 Djemba-Djemba (Off) Bellion (On)

81 ⬛ **Knight (Ung Conduct)**

86 🔄 **Boa Morte (Off) Hayles (On)**

FULL TIME 1-3

Luis Boa Morte almost connected with a header in front of goal as we continued to dominate.

Forlan shot across the face of goal, but whenever United began to exert pressure, they were undone by the fluidity of our sweeping counter-attacks.

We went close in the 28th minute, Louis Saha swivelling between Rio Ferdinand and Silvestre before firing a left-foot shot which Tim Howard parried.

Saha then went inches wide with a free header off Clark's right-wing cross.

Forlan grabbed an undeserved equaliser deep into first half stoppage time when he raced onto a Ryan Giggs through-ball and shot home to Edwin van der Sar's right.

Forlan should have scored his second in the 54th minute when he sprang our offside trap, only to shoot horribly wide.

We moved back in front on 66 minutes.

Ferdinand failed to clear Boa Morte's left-wing cross and Quinton Fortune deflected the ball into the path of Malbranque, who drove a low shot past Howard.

And the sensational Malbranque was involved once again on 79 minutes, knocking an inch-perfect through-ball to Inamoto, who swept majestically over Howard to seal a wonderful win.

"Every one of my players was different class today, and I can't pick anyone out - they were all brilliant." Chris Coleman

Statistics

Man Utd			Fulham	
This Season	This Fixture		This Fixture	This Season
64	5	Shots On Target	7	54
51	10	Shots Off Target	7	54
4	0	Hit Woodwork	1	4
41	6	Caught Offside	2	22
54	10	Corners	2	41
124	11	Fouls	18	158
49%	58%	Possession	42%	38%

League Standings

Pos (pos before)	W	D	L	F	A	Pts
3 (2) Man Utd	7	1	2	18	6	22
5 (6) Fulham	5	3	2	20	13	18

October Review

Month in Numbers

Games Played: **4**
Games Won: **2**
Games Drawn: **1**
Games Lost: **1**
Goals For: **7**
Goals Against: **4**

Results this Month

Premiership, 04/10/2003
Fulham 2-0 Leicester

Premiership, 18/10/2003
Fulham 0-0 Wolves

Premiership, 21/10/2003
Fulham 2-3 Newcastle

Premiership, 25/10/2003
Man Utd 1-3 Fulham

Premiership Table

Pos	(Sep)		Pl	W	D	L	F	A	Diff	Pts
1	(1)	Arsenal	10	7	3	0	19	8	+11	24
2	(2)	Chelsea	10	7	2	1	20	9	+11	23
3	(3)	Man Utd	10	7	1	2	18	6	+12	22
4	(4)	Birmingham	10	5	4	1	9	5	+4	19
5	**(7)**	**Fulham**	**10**	**5**	**3**	**2**	**20**	**13**	**+7**	**18**
6	(6)	Southampton	10	4	4	2	10	5	+5	16
7	(5)	Man City	10	4	3	3	20	12	+8	15
8	(19)	Newcastle	10	4	3	3	15	12	+3	15
9	(12)	Charlton	10	4	3	3	14	13	+1	15
10	(8)	Liverpool	10	4	2	4	15	11	+4	14
11	(9)	Portsmouth	10	3	3	4	11	12	-1	12
12	(17)	Tottenham	10	3	3	4	10	13	-3	12
13	(10)	Everton	10	2	4	4	12	14	-2	10
14	(13)	Aston Villa	10	2	4	4	8	12	-4	10
15	(20)	Wolves	10	2	3	5	7	21	-14	9
16	(11)	Blackburn	10	2	2	6	15	19	-4	8
17	(14)	Middlesbro'	10	2	2	6	7	15	-8	8
18	(15)	Bolton	10	1	5	4	8	19	-11	8
19	(18)	Leeds	10	2	2	6	9	21	-12	8
20	(16)	Leicester	10	1	2	7	14	21	-7	5

Premiership Progression

Win: ■ Draw: ■ Loss: ■ League position: 🔵 League position 2002-03: ⚪ Home fixtures in black

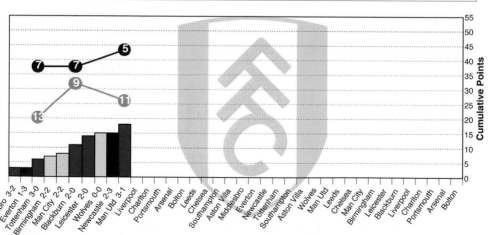

October Review

Premiership Performance

	Oct	03-04
Shots On Target	21	54
Shots Off Target	21	54
Hit Woodwork	3	4
Clean Sheets	2	4
Failed To Score	1	1
Caught Offside	14	22
Corners	13	41
Own Goals For	0	0
Own Goals Against	0	1

Goals Resulting From

	Oct		03-04	
	F	A	F	A
Open Play	7	2	18	8
Set Piece	0	2	2	4

How Goals Scored

	Oct		03-04	
	F	A	F	A
Right Foot	2	2	11	5
Left Foot	5	1	9	5
Header	0	1	0	2

When Goals Scored

	Oct		03-04	
	F	A	F	A
First Half	4	2	8	7
Second Half	3	2	12	5

Top Goal Scorers

	Oct	03-04
L. Saha	1	5
L. Boa Morte	2	5
B. Hayles	0	3
J. Inamoto	1	2
S. Malbranque	1	2
L. Clark	2	2

Top Goal Assists

	Oct	03-04
S. Malbranque	5	9
L. Saha	1	4
L. Clark	0	2
J. Bonnissel	0	1
J. Inamoto	0	1
S. Legwinski	1	1
B. Hayles	0	1
L. Boa Morte	0	1

Player of the Month

Steed Malbranque

Goals: **1** Assists: **5**

An incredible month saw the young Frenchman play a vital role in six of the seven goals scored by Fulham. He began by teeing up both of Luis Boa Morte's strikes in the victory against Leicester. Two disappointing home results followed, though the creative midfielder still conjured up an assist. However, it was in the trip to Old Trafford that he really stole the show, scoring once and setting up the other two goals in a memorable 3-1 win. By the end of October, Malbranque was the Premiership's leading assistor.

Match Details

Premiership
Sunday 2nd November 2003
Venue: Loftus Road
Attendance: 17,682
Referee: R.Styles

Premiership Fixture History

Pl:3 Draws:0	Wins ☉	■	■
Fulham	1	4	5	2
Liverpool	2	6	4	0

Starting Line-up

Crossley
Volz — Knight — Melville (c) — Bonnissel
Clark — Legwinski — Pembridge
Malbranque — Boa Morte
Saha

Heskey — Owen
Kewell — Smicer — Gerrard (c) — Murphy
Traore — Hyypia — Biscan — Finnan
Dudek

Djetou, Hayles, S.Davis, Buari, Beasant.

Henchoz, Le Tallec, Hamann, Kirkland, Sinama-Pongolle.

Luis Boa Morte holds off Vladimir Smicer

Fulham 1
Liverpool 2

A late Danny Murphy penalty denied us the chance to move into the top four, as we lost at Loftus Road for the second successive time.

Sami Hyypia spared Jerzy Dudek's blushes on 10 minutes.

The Reds' keeper lost his footing outside the box while attempting to intercept Steed Malbranque's long ball towards Louis Saha, whose scuffed shot at goal was blocked by Hyypia.

The Merseysiders then powered into the lead with a stunning strike from Emile Heskey on 17 minutes.

Liverpool's former Fulham right-back Steve Finnan drilled a left-foot cross into the box and Heskey, arriving ahead of Andy Melville, slammed the ball into the back of the net with a sweet first-time volley. It was the England frontman's fifth strike of the season.

We continued to press and grabbed an equaliser five minutes before the break.

Moritz Volz outpaced Djimi Traore on the right flank and Malbranque nipped in to cross, the ball deflecting off Steven Gerrard's leg straight to Saha, who converted with ease from five yards.

On the stroke of half-time, Saha cut in from the right and forced Dudek to scramble across his goal to make a save at the foot of his left-hand post.

Only a stunning save by Dudek denied Saha his second of the game four minutes after the interval, as Harry Kewell's clearance cannoned off Lee Clark and Saha lashed a ferocious volley which Dudek managed to get a hand to.

We almost went behind in the 64th minute, but Mark Crossley — in for the injured Edwin van der Sar — saved bravely at the feet of Vladimir Smicer and Heskey's acute follow-up effort spun wide off the heels of Jerome Bonnissel.

Crossley was the hero again as the contest ticked into the final 20 minutes.

Smicer charged onto a through-ball, hitting a shot which deflected off Bonnissel and brought the best out of Crossley, who stretched out a hand to palm the ball over the bar.

And there was late drama, as Zat Knight's rash challenge on Liverpool substitute Florent Sinama-Pongolle gave away the decisive penalty.

Murphy made no mistake from the spot, sending Crossley the wrong way as he slotted home the winner.

"It was a stone-wall penalty... And the sending-off - it was an horrendous challenge by Luis. I'll back up my players any time, but I was glad to see their player get up, because it could have been a lot more serious." Chris Coleman

Event Line

17 ⊙ Heskey (Open Play)

21 ⇄ Pembridge (Off) Djetou (On)

40 ⊙ Saha (Open Play)

HALF TIME 1-1

54 ▮ Murphy (Foul)

66 ⇄ Biscan (Off) Henchoz (On)

77 ⇄ Owen (Off) Sinama-Pongolle (On)

82 ⇄ Heskey (Off) Le Tallec (On)

86 ⇄ Saha (Off) Hayles (On)

88 ▮ Boa Morte (Dissent)

89 ⊙ Murphy (Penalty)

90 ▮ Boa Morte (Foul)

FULL TIME 1-2

Statistics

Fulham			Liverpool
This Season	This Fixture		This Fixture	This Season
59	5	Shots On Target	6	81
59	5	Shots Off Target	6	92
4	0	Hit Woodwork	0	2
25	3	Caught Offside	9	38
45	4	Corners	8	82
173	15	Fouls	10	124
39%	55%	Possession	45%	48%

League Standings

Pos (pos before)	W	D	L	F	A	Pts
6 (6) Fulham	5	3	3	21	15	18
7 (10) Liverpool	5	2	4	17	12	17

Premiership Milestone

100 Luis Boa Morte made his 100th Premiership appearance, while summer-signing Mark Crossley made his 1st Premiership appearance for Fulham.

Mark Pembridge chased by Liverpools Danny Murphy

Charlton Athletic 3
Fulham 1

A brace from Jonatan Johansson consigned us to our first Premiership loss to Charlton.

Louis Saha spun Mark Fish and tested home keeper Dean Kiely before the side from south of the river went in front with ten minutes on the clock.

After Claus Jensen set up Johansson, Edwin van der Sar parried his shot straight into the path of Graham Stuart, who swept home from eight yards for his first goal in 22 months.

Charlton upped the pressure and Scott Parker had two cracks at goal, one a sensational 40-yard strike which flew inches over the bar, the other a volley which dipped just wide.

Saha had a chance to pull us level after 26 minutes, as he raced after Luis Boa Morte's through-ball and reached it ahead of Kiely. But he stumbled as he skipped past the keeper and the opportunity was lost.

Junichi Inamoto went close to an audacious equaliser moments later, thumping a looping shot from fully 45 yards which landed on the roof of Kiely's net.

Kiely then clawed Zat Knight's header to safety before van der Sar stretched to fingertip Johansson's cross away from Kevin Lisbie at the far post.

Match Details

Premiership
Saturday 8th November 2003
Venue: The Valley
Attendance: 26,344
Referee: A.P.D'Urso

Premiership Fixture History

Pl:3 Draws:1	Wins ⊙	■	■
Charlton Athletic	1	4	5	1
Fulham	1	3	5	0

Starting Line-up

Kiely
Kishishev Perry Fish Hreidarsson
Stuart Holland Parker Jensen
Lisbie Johansson
Saha
Malbranque
Boa Morte Clark Legwinski Inamoto
Bonnissel Melville (c) Knight Volz
van der Sar

Euell, Powell, Di Canio, Sankofa, Royce.
Hayles, S.Davis, Pratley, Djetou, Crossley.

Junichi Inamoto takes on Graham Stuart

Sean Davis scores past Dean Kiely.

Event Line

10 ⊙ Stuart (Open Play)

29 ▮ Perry (Foul)

39 ⚽ Jensen (Off) Euell (On)

42 ▮ Inamoto (Foul)

HALF TIME 1-0

62 ⚽ Boa Morte (Off) Hayles (On)

66 ▮ Legwinski (Foul)

69 ⊙ Johansson (Open Play)

70 ⚽ Inamoto (Off) Davis S (On)

74 ⚽ Hayles (Off) Pratley (On)

76 ⊙ Johansson (Open Play)

80 ⚽ Parker (Off) Powell (On)

85 ⚽ Lisbie (Off) Di Canio (On)

89 ⊙ Davis S (Indirect Free Kick)

FULL TIME 3-1

We forged a decent opportunity on 54 minutes, as Moritz Volz's cross was only half cleared by Radostin Kishishev and Lee Clark thumped an angled volley into Kiely's midriff.

Van der Sar kept us in it when he dropped smartly to his right to deny Lisbie's header from a Charlton set-piece.

But the Addicks powered into a two-goal lead with a stunning Johansson strike on 69 minutes.

Jason Euell collected Johansson's header 10 yards from goal and cushioned the ball back to the Finn, who fired a thunderous half-volley past van der Sar and into the far corner. It was Johansson's first goal since March.

An error by Andy Melville gift-wrapped Charlton their third after 76 minutes.

He attempted to side-foot the ball back to van der Sar, but seriously under-hit it, allowing Johansson to poke home his second.

Charlton were rampant now and only the post prevented Euell from adding a fourth with a fierce drive.

Substitute Sean Davis – making his first appearance of the season – grabbed us an 89th minute consolation after Sylvain Legwinski's shot hit both posts.

"We could have no complaints about the result, and deserved to get beaten. The players know it. I didn't have to tell them that we weren't good enough." Chris Coleman

Statistics

Charlton			**Fulham**	
This Season	This Fixture		This Fixture	This Season
59	6	Shots On Target	6	65
61	5	Shots Off Target	6	65
2	1	Hit Woodwork	1	5
38	5	Caught Offside	0	25
55	1	Corners	5	50
175	10	Fouls	11	184
43%	49%	Possession	51%	40%

League Standings

Pos (pos before)	W	D	L	F	A	Pts
4 (7) Charlton	6	3	3	19	15	21
7 (6) Fulham	5	3	4	22	18	18

Premiership Milestone

Fulham substitute Darren Pratley made his Premiership debut.

Fulham 2
Portsmouth 0

Two goals in three minutes from Louis Saha clinched the win against Portsmouth and moved us into fifth place.

Portsmouth came to Loftus Road on the back of their 6-1 thrashing of Leeds a fortnight ago, but while goals were easy to come by at home, they had gone more than five and a half hours since their last away strike when skipper Teddy Sheringham scored at Arsenal on September 13.

That drought almost ended in the 16th minute.

Patrik Berger curled in a corner from the right and defender Dejan Stefanovic powered a downward header from eight yards which Jerome Bonnissel blocked on the line with his chest.

The visitors went close again in the 21st minute when Steve Stone's chip forward opened up space for Aiyegbeni Yakubu on the right edge of the area. But he delayed his shot and Edwin van der Sar saved at his feet.

On the half-hour, Berger conceded a free kick for a foul on Moritz Volz. The lofted ball into the box wasn't properly cleared, Hayden Foxe heading down right to Saha, who fired home from 16 yards for our 100th Premiership goal.

Match Details

Premiership
Monday 24th November 2003
Venue: Loftus Road
Attendance: 15,624
Referee: A.G.Wiley

Premiership Fixture History

	Pl:1 Draws:0	Wins ⚽	⬛	⬛
Fulham	1	2	0	0
Portsmouth	0	0	3	1

Starting Line-up

van der Sar
Volz   Knight   Melville (c)   Bonnissel
S.Davis   Legwinski   Clark
Malbranque   Hayles
Saha
Yakubu   Sheringham (c)
Berger   O'Neil   Sherwood   Stone
De Zeeuw   Stefanovic   Foxe   Schemmel
Wapenaar

Inamoto, Sava, Djetou, Pratley, Crossley.

Taylor, Smertin, Burton, Zivkovic, Srnicek.

Jerome Bonnissel and Deon Burton

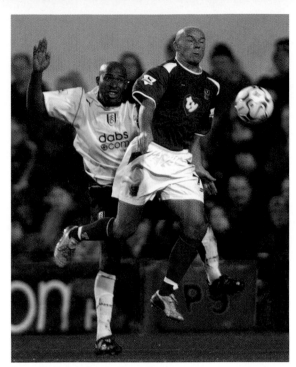

Barry Hayles challenges Steve Stone

Event Line

30 ⊙ **Saha (Open Play)**

33 ⊙ **Saha (Open Play)**

37 ■ Stone (Foul)

45 ■ Schemmel (Foul)

HALF TIME 2-0

60 ⇄ Foxe (Off) Taylor (On)

60 ⇄ O'Neil (Off) Smertin (On)

68 ⇄ **Hayles (Off) Inamoto (On)**

70 ■ Sherwood (Foul)

70 ⇄ **Saha (Off) Sava (On)**

73 ⇄ Stone (Off) Burton (On)

82 ■ Berger (Dissent)

FULL TIME 2-0

Three minutes later, Lee Clark crossed from the right and Saha nipped ahead of Foxe on the six yard line to power home a header for his eighth goal of the season.

The second half wasn't much of a spectacle, with the quality of passing pretty poor by Premiership standards.

Pompey boss Harry Redknapp reshuffled, sending on Matt Taylor, Alexei Smertin and Deon Burton, but the visitors never really threatened.

Saha was withdrawn on 70 minutes due to concern over a slight hamstring injury and was replaced by Facundo Sava, who was unfortunate not to add a third to our tally when his header off Clark's cross crashed against the bar on 79 minutes.

Stone, Sebastien Schemmel and Tim Sherwood all picked up yellow cards as indiscipline began to creep into Pompey's game.

Pompey's fate was finally sealed on 82 minutes when Berger was sent off after complaining to Alan Wiley over the referee's decision not to award a penalty for Zat Knight's challenge on Yakubu.

Statistics

Fulham			Portsmouth	
This Season	This Fixture		This Fixture	This Season
68	3	Shots On Target	6	54
70	5	Shots Off Target	6	68
6	1	Hit Woodwork	0	2
27	2	Caught Offside	1	44
52	2	Corners	11	65
194	10	Fouls	16	225
41%	50%	Possession	50%	46%

League Standings

Pos (pos before)	W	D	L	F	A	Pts
5 (7) Fulham	6	3	4	24	18	21
11 (11) Portsmouth	4	3	6	17	18	15

Premiership Milestone

100 Louis Saha's goal after half an hour was Fulham's 100th in the Premiership.

"For the first 25 minutes we were second best all round and they had a few chances to score, but we dug in and stuck together"
Chris Coleman

Arsenal 0
Fulham 0

Edwin van der Sar proved too big an obstacle for Arsenal, as we earned a valuable point at Highbury.

The Arsenal onslaught began in the sixth minute.

Dennis Bergkamp fed Thierry Henry, who won a corner on the left. Henry sent in the cross, Pascal Cygan flicked it on at the near post and the ball came off the boot of Kolo Toure, but flew just over the bar.

Bergkamp picked out Freddie Ljungberg's run with a 40-yard pass into our box on 16 minutes.

The Swede tried to lift the ball over the keeper, but van der Sar managed to deflect it to safety with an outstretched arm.

Robert Pires wasted a great chance four minutes later, shooting wide from eight yards after fellow Frenchman Henry had teed him up.

Pires made amends with some magical skill in the 30th minute, as he ghosted past two defenders to return the compliment for Henry, but van der Sar dived to his right to beat away his side-footed shot.

Match Details

Premiership
Sunday 30th November 2003
Venue: Highbury
Attendance: 38,063
Referee:G.P.Barber

Premiership Fixture History

Pl:**3** Draws:**1**	Wins	⊙	■	■
Arsenal	2	6	4	0
Fulham	**0**	**2**	**3**	**0**

Starting Line-up

Lehmann
Toure Campbell Cygan Cole
Ljungberg Gilberto Edu Pires
Bergkamp (c) Henry
Saha
Malbranque Inamoto
Clark Legwinski S.Davis
Bonnissel Melville (c) Knight Volz
van der Sar

Kanu, Aliadiere, Hoyte, Clichy, Stack.

Hayles, Goma, Djetou, Sava, Crossley.

Nwankwo Kanu is challenged by Jerome Bonnissel

Edwin van der Sar keeps his eyes on the ball

Event Line

HALF TIME 0-0

57 ▌ **Legwinski (Foul)**

67 ⮂ Gilberto (Off) Kanu (On)

76 ⮂ **Saha (Off) Hayles (On)**

79 ⮂ Ljungberg (Off) Aliadiere (On)

90 ▌ Edu (Foul)

FULL TIME 0-0

Statistics

Arsenal			Fulham	
This Season	This Fixture		This Fixture	This Season
87	12	Shots On Target	0	68
81	10	Shots Off Target	6	76
7	0	Hit Woodwork	0	6
46	3	Caught Offside	4	31
73	9	Corners	0	52
189	14	Fouls	11	205
51%	56%	Possession	44%	41%

League Standings

Pos (pos before)		W	D	L	F	A	Pts
2 (1)	Arsenal	10	4	0	28	10	34
4 (5)	Fulham	6	4	4	24	18	22

Arsenal kept up the pressure and after 32 minutes van der Sar was called upon to save us once again, this time diving to his left to keep out Bergkamp's 20-yard effort.

It was turning into a bit of a one-man show, as a minute later the Dutch keeper produced a similar stop to deny Henry.

Arsenal picked up where they'd left off as the second half got underway, Pires feeding Henry, whose low cross from the left was just too far for Gilberto to reach as he raced in.

Van der Sar then made another vital save to deny Bergkamp's shot from inside the box.

Arsenal went close yet again on 61 minutes when Ashley Cole's long ball out of defence picked out Bergkamp on the right edge of the box.

The skipper brought it under control before drilling a low shot which van der Sar saved with his legs.

The loose ball fell to Ljungberg, but his effort lacked the power to seriously trouble the keeper.

Arsenal were caught napping on 66 minutes and were lucky to escape, as Sean Davis' cross from the right found Steed Malbranque, who sent a free header wide of the near post.

"I've probably never had a busier 90 minutes. I enjoyed it." Edwin van der Sar

November Review

Month in Numbers

Games Played: **4**
Games Won: **1**
Games Drawn: **1**
Games Lost: **2**
Goals For: **4**
Goals Against: **5**

Results this Month

Premiership, 02/11/2003
Fulham 1-2 Liverpool

Premiership, 08/11/2003
Charlton 3-1 Fulham

Premiership, 24/11/2003
Fulham 2-0 Portsmouth

Premiership, 30/11/2003
Arsenal 0-0 Fulham

Premiership Table

Pos	(Oct)		Pl	W	D	L	F	A	Diff	Pts
1	(2)	Chelsea	14	11	2	1	28	9	+19	35
2	(1)	Arsenal	14	10	4	0	28	10	+18	34
3	(3)	Man Utd	14	10	1	3	25	9	+16	31
4	**(5)**	**Fulham**	**14**	**6**	**4**	**4**	**24**	**18**	**+6**	**22**
5	(9)	Charlton	14	6	4	4	20	17	+3	22
6	(10)	Liverpool	14	6	3	5	21	15	+6	21
7	(8)	Newcastle	14	5	5	4	20	19	+1	20
8	(4)	Birmingham	14	5	5	4	12	14	-2	20
9	(7)	Man City	14	5	3	6	22	19	+3	18
10	(17)	Middlesbro'	14	5	3	6	12	15	-3	18
11	(18)	Bolton	14	4	6	4	13	19	-6	18
12	(6)	Southampton	14	4	5	5	10	9	+1	17
13	(20)	Leicester	14	4	3	7	22	22	0	15
14	(11)	Portsmouth	14	4	3	7	17	20	-3	15
15	(12)	Tottenham	14	4	3	7	13	18	-5	15
16	(16)	Blackburn	14	4	2	8	19	24	-5	14
17	(14)	Aston Villa	14	3	5	6	11	17	-6	14
18	(13)	Everton	14	3	4	7	15	19	-4	13
19	(15)	Wolves	14	2	5	7	9	27	-18	11
20	(19)	Leeds	14	3	2	9	12	33	-21	11

Premiership Progression

Win:■ Draw:■ Loss:■ League position: **8** League position 2002-03: **8** Home fixtures in black

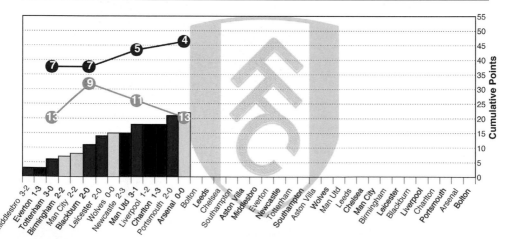

November Review

	Nov	03-04
Shots On Target	**14**	68
Shots Off Target	**22**	76
Hit Woodwork	**2**	6
Clean Sheets	**2**	6
Failed To Score	**1**	2
Caught Offside	**9**	31
Corners	**11**	52
Own Goals For	**0**	0
Own Goals Against	**0**	1

Goals Resulting From

	Nov		03-04	
	F	**A**	F	A
Open Play	**3**	**4**	21	12
Set Piece	**1**	**1**	3	5

How Goals Scored

	Nov		03-04	
	F	**A**	F	A
Right Foot	**0**	**4**	11	9
Left Foot	**3**	**1**	12	6
Header	**1**	**0**	1	2

When Goals Scored

	Nov		03-04	
	F	**A**	F	A
First Half	**3**	**2**	11	9
Second Half	**1**	**3**	13	8

Top Goal Scorers

	Nov	03-04
L. Saha	**3**	8
L. Boa Morte	**0**	5
B. Hayles	**0**	3
J. Inamoto	**0**	2
S. Malbranque	**0**	2
L. Clark	**0**	2

Top Goal Assists

	Nov	03-04
S.Malbranque	**0**	9
L. Saha	**0**	4
L. Clark	**1**	3
S. Legwinski	**1**	2
J. Bonnissel	**0**	1
J. Inamoto	**0**	1
B. Hayles	**0**	1
L. Boa Morte	**0**	1

Edwin van der Sar

Clean sheets: **2**

Having missed the home defeat to Liverpool, van der Sar had an uncomfortable return to action in a 3-1 loss at Charlton. The tall Dutch keeper put that result behind him to record a clean sheet against Portsmouth, a game in which he had his work cut out in the early stages. Then came proof that he was still one of the finest in the world, as he almost single-handedly kept a rampant Arsenal side at bay at Highbury. The Gunners bombarded the goal, but none of their 12 efforts on target found a way through.

Fulham 2
Bolton Wanderers 1

A late goal from Argentinian striker Facundo Sava earned us a sensational win over Bolton at Loftus Road which kept us in fourth place.

Sava netted 14 minutes from time, just 60 seconds after Sean Davis had cancelled out Kevin Davies' 53rd-minute opener for Wanderers.

Wanderers went close after just 10 seconds, as Simon Charlton's long ball was flicked on by Davies to Kevin Nolan, whose shot was tipped round the post by Edwin van der Sar.

Lee Clark had our first shot at goal after 22 minutes, but he blasted his first-time swipe into the stand from an excellent position after tenacious work by Junichi Inamoto.

Wanderers hit back with a close-range attempt from Youri Djorkaeff which van der Sar handled comfortably.

Nolan's acrobatics almost created the first goal, as he chested a bouncing ball above his head and smacked an overhead kick goalwards.

Van der Sar spilt the ball after the initial save, but managed to gather before Ivan Campo could smash home the rebound.

Inamoto fluffed our clearest opening of the first 45 minutes, thrashing the ball wide when clean through after racing onto

Match Details

Premiership
Saturday 6th December 2003
Venue: Loftus Road
Attendance: 14,393
Referee: A.P.D'Urso

Premiership Fixture History

	Pl: 3	Draws: 0	Wins ⊙	■	■
Fulham	3	9	1	0
Bolton Wanderers	0	2	4	0

Starting Line-up

van der Sar

Volz Knight Melville (c) Bonnissel

S.Davis Legwinski Clark

Inamoto Malbranque

Saha

Davies

Djorkaeff Nolan

Okocha (c) Campo Frandsen

Gardner Charlton N'Gotty Hunt

Jaaskelainen

Hayles, Sava, Djetou, Goma, Crossley.

Jardel, Ba, Stelios, Thome, Poole.

Steed Malbranque being chased by Nicky Hunt

Andy Melville and Kevin Davies in action

Event Line

22 ▉ Gardner (Ung Conduct)

HALF TIME 0-0

50 ▉ Frandsen (Ung Conduct)

51 ⇄ Saha (Off) Hayles (On)

53 ⚽ Davies (Open Play)

58 ⇄ Inamoto (Off) Sava (On)

75 ⚽ Davis S (Open Play)

76 ⚽ Sava (Open Play)

81 ⇄ Davis S (Off) Djetou (On)

81 ⇄ Frandsen (Off) Stelios (On)

85 ⇄ Nolan (Off) Jardel (On)

89 ⇄ Campo (Off) Ba (On)

FULL TIME 2-1

Statistics

Fulham			Bolton	
This Season	This Fixture		This Fixture	This Season
72	4	Shots On Target	6	81
82	6	Shots Off Target	6	106
7	1	Hit Woodwork	0	6
39	8	Caught Offside	4	43
55	3	Corners	2	92
220	15	Fouls	15	205
42%	60%	Possession	40%	43%

League Standings

Pos (pos before)		W	D	L	F	A	Pts
4 (4)	Fulham	7	4	4	26	19	25
12 (11)	Bolton	4	6	5	14	21	18

Premiership Milestone

25 The game saw Kevin Davies' 25th Premiership goal.

Louis Saha's excellent pass.

Wanderers broke the deadlock eight minutes after the break, as Jay-Jay Okocha's long throw from the right was flicked on by Campo for Davies to slam home with a close-range volley.

Davies should have doubled Wanderers' advantage a minute later, but he made a complete hash of Ricardo Gardner's cross, sending a header bouncing into the turf and onto the roof of the net.

We forced our way back into the game and could have grabbed an equaliser when Sava, who had come on for Inamoto, headed against the woodwork.

But we didn't have to wait long to get back on level terms, as Barry Hayles squared for Davis, who thumped the ball into the back of the net from 12 yards.

And it was 2-1 just a minute later, as Gardner unintentionally diverted a loose ball into the path of Sava, who swept it into the bottom-right corner.

We had to survive some drama deep into injury time when Wanderers substitute Mario Jardel went close with a header.

"We know we were fortunate. We were poor for 75 minutes and Bolton were 1-0 up and deserved to be. But we had a lot of strong characters out there, kept fighting and scrapping, and got our reward."
Chris Coleman

Leeds United 3
Fulham 2

Dominic Matteo fired a last-gasp winner to give Leeds their first Elland Road victory for more than two months.

Louis Saha looked to have salvaged a point for us after he grabbed a second-half brace to cancel out Leeds' advantage. But moments after his 86th minute second goal, Leeds skipper Matteo was left unmarked to head home his first for three years.

On 41 minutes, Ian Harte fired a 20-yard free kick which van der Sar parried brilliantly, but unfortunately straight at Michael Duberry, who shinned the ball home - the look on his face suggesting he was as stunned as everyone else that he'd scored.

Leeds opened up a two-goal cushion just 45 seconds after the restart, courtesy of Mark Viduka's third of the season. A James Milner throw found Viduka with his back to goal 25 yards out, and after first holding off the challenge of Zat Knight, he left van der Sar rooted to his line with a superb right-foot curler.

Match Details

Premiership
Sunday 14th December 2003
Venue: Elland Road
Attendance: 30,544
Referee: N.S.Barry

Premiership Fixture History

	Pl	Draws	Wins ☉	■	■
Leeds United	3	0	2 5	4	0
Fulham		1	3	6	0

Starting Line-up

Robinson
Kelly Duberry Radebe Harte
Smith Batty Matteo (c)
Pennant Milner
Viduka
Saha
Boa Morte Malbranque
Clark Legwinski S.Davis
Harley Melville (c) Knight Volz
van der Sar

Richardson, Morris, McPhail, Bridges, Carson.
Hayles, Sava, Goma, Djetou, Crossley.

Louis Saha is chased by Dominic Matteo and Mark Viduka.

But 70 seconds later we were back in the game - Sean Davis fed the ball to Saha, and although there appeared no danger from 25 yards, his raking right-foot shot flew beyond the outstretched reach of Paul Robinson for his ninth of the season.

We almost tied it up in the 57th minute, but Robinson displayed exceptional reflexes to beat away a 15-yard half-volley from Saha off Davis' corner.

On-loan Arsenal winger Jermaine Pennant went close for Leeds 90 seconds later, turning inside skipper Andy Melville before striking the bar with a cracking left-foot shot.

We were fortunate again 12 minutes from time, as a right-wing cross from Pennant deflected off Melville, with Milner firing the chance over.

A Milner curler was saved by van der Sar before Saha looked to have earned us a share of the spoils with a 20-yard drive which spun in off the left hand of Robinson with four minutes to go.

But Matteo would have the last word, timing his run perfectly to head home Harte's free kick.

"I think last week we were probably a little bit fortunate to get three points, but we were unfortunate today. We knew it was going to be a hard game ... Leeds battled really hard and fought for every tackle."
Chris Coleman

Fulham's Jon Harley is challenged by Alan Smith of Leeds.

Event Line

41 ⚽ Duberry (Indirect Free Kick)

HALF TIME 1-0

46 ⚽ Viduka (Open Play)

47 ⚽ Saha (Open Play)

52 ▮ Boa Morte (Dissent)

56 ▮ Batty (Foul)

62 ▮ Smith (Ung Conduct)

63 🔁 Volz (Off) Hayles (On)

77 🔁 Boa Morte (Off) Sava (On)

86 ⚽ Saha (Open Play)

88 ⚽ Matteo (Indirect Free Kick)

FULL TIME 3-2

Statistics

| Leeds | | | Fulham | |
This Season	This Fixture		This Fixture	This Season
63	8	Shots On Target	5	77
73	4	Shots Off Target	3	85
2	1	Hit Woodwork	0	7
45	2	Caught Offside	2	41
66	6	Corners	5	60
256	16	Fouls	13	233
43%	44%	Possession	56%	43%

League Standings

Pos (pos before)		W	D	L	F	A	Pts
19 (19)	Leeds	4	3	9	16	36	15
4 (4)	Fulham	7	4	5	28	22	25

Fulham 0
Chelsea 1

Match Details

Premiership
Saturday 20th December 2003
Venue: Loftus Road
Attendance: 18,244
Referee: M.A.Riley

Premiership Fixture History

Pl:**3** Draws:**2**	Wins	⚽	■	■
Fulham	0	1	4	0
Chelsea	1	2	6	1

Starting Line-up

van der Sar

Volz   Knight   Melville (c)   Harley

Clark   Legwinski   S.Davis

Malbranque   Boa Morte

Saha

Mutu   Crespo

Duff   Lampard   Makelele   Gronkjaer

Bridge   Desailly (c)   Terry   Johnson

Cudicini

Djetou, Hayles,
Goma, Sava,
Crossley.

J.Cole, Geremi,
Gallas, Melchiot,
Sullivan.

Moritz Volz and Joe Cole in action

A bullet header from Hernan Crespo led Chelsea past us in a pulsating London derby.

We started brightly, Carlo Cudicini saving Louis Saha's header after two minutes, then seizing Andy Melville's flicked header just below his crossbar.

At the other end, Damien Duff forced an excellent save from Edwin van der Sar with a 20-yard effort.

The visitors could have taken the lead in the 12th minute when Crespo broke into space, but he poked his shot wide under pressure from Melville.

Chelsea were beginning to gain the upper hand, as Joe Cole fed Adrian Mutu, who stung van der Sar's palms with an angled drive. Chelsea twice went close to the opener in the 32nd minute.

Steed Malbranque's clearance rebounded off Glen Johnson and Jon Harley headed over his crossbar as the ball threatened to bounce in.

Crespo then cleverly diverted a near-post corner back to the penalty spot for John Terry, whose strike was smartly blocked by van der Sar right on his line.

Cudicini made a superb save off Melville's powerful header on the stroke of half-time.

Zat Knight challenges Adrian Mutu

Event Line

8 Duff (Off) Cole (On)

34 Cole (Foul)

37 Davis S (Off) Djetou (On)

45 Johnson (Foul)

HALF TIME 0-0

62 Crespo (Open Play)

69 Harley (Off) Hayles (On)

76 Saha (Foul)

84 Cole (Off) Geremi (On)

84 Gronkjaer (Foul)

88 Clark (Foul)

89 Crespo (Off) Gallas (On)

FULL TIME 0-1

Statistics

Fulham			Chelsea	
This Season	This Fixture		This Fixture	This Season
83	6	Shots On Target	10	92
90	5	Shots Off Target	2	103
7	0	Hit Woodwork	0	2
41	0	Caught Offside	5	57
62	2	Corners	8	96
248	15	Fouls	16	245
43%	39%	Possession	61%	53%

League Standings

Pos (pos before)		W	D	L	F	A	Pts
4 (4)	Fulham	7	4	6	28	23	25
2 (3)	Chelsea	12	3	2	31	12	39

Chelsea fashioned a great opening six minutes after the break and should have taken the lead.

Cole skipped away from a challenge and slipped a fine pass in behind Melville.

Crespo raced onto it and squared for Frank Lampard, but the midfielder scuffed his shot and van der Sar saved well at the foot of his left-hand post.

But the Dutch keeper was powerless to prevent the visitors seizing the lead after 62 minutes.

Wayne Bridge fired over a cross from the left and Crespo towered above Melville to thump a header into the top corner.

Cudicini had luck on his side four minutes later, as Luis Boa Morte raced into the area and fired a shot which beat the Italian keeper's dive before hitting his boot and rebounding into his grasp.

Cudicini then fisted away Malbranque's deflected 25-yard piledriver, while van der Sar had to be alert to save a fierce drive from Cole and block Lampard's close-range effort.

Late on, right-back Moritz Volz sent a 25-yarder fizzing a foot over the top.

"We made a few chances, but our general play was poor. We looked like we were panicking at times and kicking it long when we could have shown better composure. But we're fourth because we're a good team and deserve to be there." Chris Coleman

Match Details

Premiership
Friday 26th December 2003
Venue: Loftus Road
Attendance: 16,767
Referee: D.J.Gallagher

Premiership Fixture History

	Pl:3 Draws:1	Wins ⚽	▇	▇
Fulham	2	6	1	0
Southampton	0	3	4	0

Starting Line-up

van der Sar
Volz · Knight · Goma · Bonnissel
Inamoto · Djetou · Clark (c)
Malbranque · Boa Morte
Saha

Beattie · Ormerod
McCann · Marsden · Prutton · Telfer
Higginbotham · Dodd (c)
M.Svensson · Lundekvam
Niemi

Harley, Melville, Hayles, Sava, Crossley.

Phillips, Delgado, Baird, A.Svensson, Blayney.

Lee Clark turns away from Saints' Chris Marsden

Fulham 2
Southampton 0

Louis Saha grabbed both goals in a comfortable win over Southampton.

He struck in the 19th minute before clinching victory with a 63rd-minute penalty which took his tally to 12 for the season.

The win – only the fourth in our last 11 league matches – lifted us back above Saints in the table.

Back-to-back defeats to Leeds and Chelsea had done nothing to dent our confidence, and we made the early running, forcing three quick corners.

Neil McCann and Michael Svensson both had efforts fly yards wide at the other end for the visitors shortly afterwards.

Saha had looked largely anonymous until he found himself in the clear on 19 minutes.

Steed Malbranque played a neat one-two with Lee Clark before releasing his fellow countryman, who made no mistake with a left-foot finish into the far corner.

Saha might have doubled the lead moments later when Luis Boa Morte's low centre found him in space again. But this time he failed to make the right contact and the chance went begging.

We were straight back into our stride as the second half

began, Saha hitting a 20-yard effort wide of the far post.

He was in again moments later, shrugging off a weak Jason Dodd challenge before knocking over a dangerous ball which eluded everyone and flashed harmlessly across the face of goal.

Malbranque then found Saha with a stunning 30-yard pass and the striker controlled with his chest before powering a right-foot volley.

It looked a certain goal until Finnish international Antti Niemi pulled off a spectacular save, the rebound falling to Junichi Inamoto, who blasted over.

Saints finally tested Edwin van der Sar on the hour, Kevin Phillips letting fly from 25 yards, only for the Dutchman to save low at his far post.

Moments later, referee Dermot Gallagher pointed to the spot after Boa Morte was tripped by Chris Marsden.

Saha stepped up and fired down the middle, the ball ricocheting through Niemi's legs and into the back of the net.

Malbranque deserved a goal for his efforts, but he contrived to miss from three yards after Zat Knight's header down from a corner, scooping the ball over the crossbar with an outstretched boot.

"We were brave and we took the game to Southampton right from the start. We played better football, we matched them in the tackle and I think today we were the team that worked the hardest."
Chris Coleman

Alain Goma is too strong for James Beattie

Event Line

19 ⊙ **Saha (Open Play)**

23 ⇄ **Bonnissel (Off) Harley (On)**

HALF TIME 1-0

51 ⇄ Ormerod (Off) Phillips (On)

63 ⊙ **Saha (Penalty)**

73 ⇄ McCann (Off) Delgado (On)

83 ▉ Svensson M (Foul)

85 ▉ Prutton (Foul)

FULL TIME 2-0

Statistics

Fulham			Southampton	
This Season	This Fixture		This Fixture	This Season
90	7	Shots On Target	2	84
97	7	Shots Off Target	4	96
7	0	Hit Woodwork	0	6
42	1	Caught Offside	5	59
73	11	Corners	6	105
265	17	Fouls	14	233
44%	58%	Possession	42%	45%

League Standings

Pos (pos before)		W	D	L	F	A	Pts
4 (5)	Fulham	8	4	6	30	23	28
7 (4)	Soton	7	5	6	18	14	26

Premiership Milestone

25 Louis Saha's 2nd strike was his 25th Premiership goal for Fulham

Match Details

Premiership
Sunday 28th December 2003
Venue: Villa Park
Attendance: 35,617
Referee: B.Knight

Premiership Fixture History

Pl:3	Draws:0	Wins		■	■
Aston Villa	3	8	4	0
Fulham	**0**	**1**	**3**	**0**

Starting Line-up

Sorensen
Delaney Mellberg (c) Johnsen Samuel
Hendrie McCann Whittingham Barry
Vassell Angel

Boa Morte Saha Malbranque
Clark (c) Djetou Inamoto
Harley Goma Knight Volz
van der Sar

Ridgewell, Crouch, S.Moore, Postma, Hitzlsperger.

Hayles, Sava, Melville, Green, Crossley.

Junichi Inamoto in action

Aston Villa 3
Fulham 0

England international Darius Vassell scored at Villa Park for the first time in nearly a year as David O'Leary's side consigned us to a comprehensive defeat.

We started brightly, but were generally unable to find the form which had lifted us to fourth in the Premiership.

It required a goal line clearance by Villa midfielder Lee Hendrie to prevent us taking the lead on three minutes. Inamoto's corner was met by the head of Alain Goma, and his effort looked destined for the corner of the net until Hendrie intervened.

Villa keeper Thomas Sorensen then produced a superb reflex save to turn over a close-range shot from Steed Malbranque after 12-goal Louis Saha had provided the telling ball across the area.

The home side responded with a close-range volley from Juan Pablo Angel which Edwin van der Sar parried around the post.

The impressive Angel broke the deadlock on 33 minutes with a typical poacher's finish. Jlloyd Samuel was the creator, running past the challenges of Malbranque and Volz before delivering a low cross for Angel to slot home at the far post. It was his 13th goal of the campaign and sixth in the last seven games.

Lee Clark is pressured by Villa's Gavin McCann

Event Line

33 ⚽ Angel (Open Play)

HALF TIME 1-0

62 🔄 Delaney (Off) Ridgewell (On)

67 ⚽ Vassell (Open Play)

69 🔄 Inamoto (Off) Hayles (On)

75 🔄 Hendrie (Off) Hitzlsperger (On)

82 ⚽ Vassell (Open Play)

82 🔄 Malbranque (Off) Sava (On)

84 🔄 Angel (Off) Moore S (On)

FULL TIME 3-0

Statistics

Aston Villa			Fulham	
This Season	This Fixture		This Fixture	This Season
81	7	Shots On Target	3	93
113	5	Shots Off Target	7	104
4	0	Hit Woodwork	0	7
84	8	Caught Offside	0	42
118	8	Corners	3	76
306	16	Fouls	7	272
44%	52%	Possession	48%	44%

League Standings

Pos (pos before)		W	D	L	F	A	Pts
10 (12)	Aston Villa	6	6	7	19	23	24
5 (4)	Fulham	8	4	7	30	26	28

The Villans then almost doubled their advantage but Mellberg's header from Gareth Barry's corner went wide.

We came out for the second half in a positive fashion, Saha trying his luck from 35 yards with a well-struck volley which flew straight at Sorensen. But Villa quickly retaliated, Vassell going within inches of connecting with a low cross from Barry which carried just too much pace.

At the other end, the sharp Saha was only a foot wide after a quickfire turn and shot from the edge of the Villa penalty area.

The stadium erupted on 67 minutes, as Vassell scored his first Premiership goal of the season and his first at home since New Year's Day. Samuel was again the creator, knocking over a deep centre for Vassell, who volleyed under the body of van der Sar.

Eight minutes from time, Vassell struck again with a similar kind of finish, the cross this time supplied by substitute Thomas Hitzlsperger.

"It's the first time I've seen that happen for a long time. It was poor. We lost all our individual battles and our passing was poor. It was a cold night and the fans who came here will be going home disappointed."
Chris Coleman

December Review

Month in Numbers

Games Played: **5**
Games Won: **2**
Games Drawn: **0**
Games Lost: **3**
Goals For: **6**
Goals Against: **8**

Results this Month

Premiership, 06/12/2003
Fulham 2-1 Bolton

Premiership, 14/12/2003
Leeds 3-2 Fulham

Premiership, 20/12/2003
Fulham 0-1 Chelsea

Premiership, 26/12/2003
Fulham 2-0 Southampton

Premiership, 28/12/2003
Aston Villa 3-0 Fulham

Premiership Table

Pos	(Nov)		Pl	W	D	L	F	A	Diff	Pts
1	(3)	Man Utd	19	15	1	3	38	13	+25	46
2	(2)	Arsenal	19	13	6	0	35	12	+23	45
3	(1)	Chelsea	19	13	3	3	36	16	+20	42
4	(5)	Charlton	19	8	6	5	27	22	+5	30
5	**(4)**	**Fulham**	**19**	**8**	**4**	**7**	**30**	**26**	**+4**	**28**
6	(6)	Liverpool	18	7	5	6	28	21	+7	26
7	(7)	Newcastle	19	6	8	5	26	22	+4	26
8	(12)	Southampton	19	7	5	7	18	15	+3	26
9	(8)	Birmingham	18	7	5	6	16	20	-4	26
10	(17)	Aston Villa	19	6	6	7	19	23	-4	24
11	(18)	Everton	19	6	5	8	23	25	-2	23
12	(11)	Bolton	19	5	8	6	20	28	-8	23
13	(9)	Man City	19	5	6	8	27	27	0	21
14	(16)	Blackburn	19	6	3	10	26	29	-3	21
15	(10)	Middlesbro'	18	5	6	7	14	18	-4	21
16	(14)	Portsmouth	19	5	4	10	20	28	-8	19
17	(13)	Leicester	19	4	6	9	28	31	-3	18
18	(15)	Tottenham	19	5	3	11	19	29	-10	18
19	(20)	Leeds	19	4	5	10	18	40	-22	17
20	(19)	Wolves	18	3	5	10	16	39	-23	14

Premiership Progression

Win:■ Draw:■ Loss:■ League position: ❽ League position 2002-03: ❽ Home fixtures in black

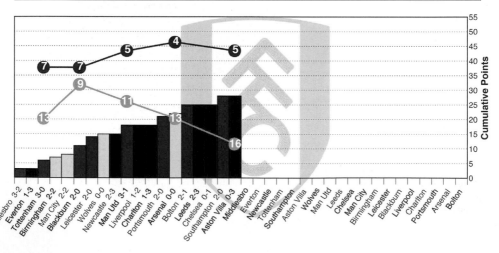

December Review

Premiership Performance

	Dec	03-04
Shots On Target	25	93
Shots Off Target	28	104
Hit Woodwork	1	7
Clean Sheets	1	7
Failed To Score	2	4
Caught Offside	11	42
Corners	24	76
Own Goals For	0	0
Own Goals Against	0	1

Goals Resulting From

	Dec		03-04	
	F	A	F	A
Open Play	5	6	26	18
Set Piece	1	2	4	7

How Goals Scored

	Dec		03-04	
	F	A	F	A
Right Foot	3	3	14	12
Left Foot	3	3	15	9
Header	0	2	1	4

When Goals Scored

	Dec		03-04	
	F	A	F	A
First Half	1	2	12	11
Second Half	5	6	18	14

Top Goal Scorers

	Dec	03-04
L. Saha	4	12
L. Boa Morte	0	5
B. Hayles	0	3
J. Inamoto	0	2
S. Malbranque	0	2
S. Davis	1	2
L. Clark	0	2

Top Goal Assists

	Dec	03-04
S. Malbranque	1	10
L. Saha	0	4
B. Hayles	2	3
L. Clark	0	3
S. Legwinski	0	2
L. Boa Morte	1	2

Player of the Month

Louis Saha

Goals: **4** Assists: **0**

A patchy month for Fulham was not reflected in the form of Louis Saha. The young French striker netted four of his side's six goals during December to move up to joint third in the Premiership scoring charts. A spectacular brace at Leeds was not quite enough to earn a point, but his two goals against Southampton on Boxing Day proved decisive. Saha had now caught the attention of Man United and in the New Year moved to The Champions for a fee in excess of £11million.

Match Details

F.A. Cup Third Round
Sunday 4th January 2004
Venue: Loftus Road
Attendance: 10, 303
Referee: P.Walton

Starting Line-up

van der Sar

Djetou   Knight   Goma   Green

S.Davis   Legwinski (c)   Inamoto

Malbranque   Petta

Saha

Spencer   Taylor

McCann   Forsyth   Finnigan (c)   Devaney

Victory   Brough   M.Duff   Wilson

Higgs

Melville, Hayles,   Odejayi, Yates,
Sava, Pratley,   Bird, S.Duff,
Crossley.   Book.

Barry Hayles takes on John Brough.

Fulham 2
Cheltenham Town 1

Louis Saha scored two goals, one in injury-time which spared us an early exit from the F.A. Cup.

It was a plucky display from the visitors, who made it clear from the start they were not intending to make up the numbers.

But no one expected the drama which unfolded in the fifth minute.

Grant McCann had plenty of time to tee up his shot from just outside the area and he made no mistake, thumping the ball into the right corner and well beyond the reach of a despairing dive by Edwin van der Sar.

But we levelled eight minutes later, as Sylvain Legwinski floated in a sublime cross to Saha, who, despite the attention of John Brough and Michael Duff, scooped his shot over the head of Shane Higgs and into the back of Cheltenham's net.

Saha could have made it two, but he nodded Steed Malbranque's cross over the bar.

Saha was proving a handful up front and with Malbranque having few problems picking out the French marksman, we were looking the more likely to score, even after Duff's header was kept out by a magnificent save from van der Sar.

Bobby Petta in the air

Event Line

5 ⚽ McCann (Open Play)

13 ⚽ Saha (Open Play)

HALF TIME 1-1

46 ⇄ Goma (Off) Melville (On)

58 ⇄ Inamoto (Off) Hayles (On)

64 ▮ Devaney (Foul)

84 ⇄ Spencer (Off) Odejayi (On)

89 ▮ Forsyth (Foul)

90 ⚽ Saha (Corner)

FULL TIME 2-1

Statistics

Fulham		Cheltenham
5	Shots On Target	5
6	Shots Off Target	4
1	Hit Woodwork	0
3	Caught Offside	2
9	Corners	2
12	Fouls	16

Malbranque and Martin Djetou attacked down the right, but Djetou's final pass lacked accuracy. Saha was then just inches short of meeting Junichi Inamoto's square ball.

Cheltenham's defence were starting to look more comfortable, forcing Saha to attempt a speculative long-range effort.

Zat Knight headed Bobby Petta's corner wide in the 56th minute before Chris Coleman sent on Barry Hayles for Inamoto to add some extra thrust up front.

The move almost paid immediate dividends when the Jamaican international just failed to meet Malbranque's dab through.

Petta went desperately close in the 67th minute when he fired a blistering shot across the face of goal, while Cheltenham captain John Finnigan slammed a powerful strike into the advertising boards.

We poured forward in the last 20 minutes as we sought the winner, and our efforts were rewarded in injury time when Petta's corner to the far post found Saha, who made no mistake with his match-winning header.

"We were truly fortunate. It was a game best forgotten." Chris Coleman

Middlesbrough 2
Fulham 1

Premiership
Wednesday 7th January 2004
Venue: Riverside Stadium
Attendance: 27,869
Referee: P.A.Durkin

Premiership Fixture History

	Pl:3	Draws:1	Wins ⚽	■	■
Middlesbrough	2	6	6	0	
Fulham	0	4	6	0	

Starting Line-up

Jones

Mills Ehiogu Southgate (c) Queudrue

Nemeth Boateng Zenden Downing

Juninho

Job

Boa Morte Saha Malbranque

S.Davis Legwinski Clark (c)

Green Melville Knight Djetou

van der Sar

Riggott, Turnbull, Parnaby, Doriva, Maccarone.

Hayles, Crossley, Hudson, Inamoto, Petta.

All the attention was meant to be on Louis Saha, but a teenage left winger called Stewart Downing stole the limelight from the French striker.

The 19-year-old was at the heart of everything good about Middlesbrough and both the home side's goals came as a result of his incisive dead-ball kicking.

Boro's early pressure told in the 15th minute when Joseph-Desire Job won a fortunate corner off Zat Knight.

Downing's kick found Ugo Ehiogu unmarked and he had time to bring the ball down and drive in a shot that Edwin van der Sar could only parry up for Job to rifle into the net.

We finally put together a good passing move, Knight finding Steed Malbranque, who quickly transferred the ball into Lee Clark's path. A goal beckoned, but Australian keeper Brad Jones, making his Premiership debut, saved with his feet to keep Boro in front.

Malbranque tested Jones again from 20 yards before the home side had two more good chances.

First, Job expertly controlled Danny Mills' long ball and struck

Lee Clark gets his head to the ball

Steed Malbranque outpaces Boudewijn Zenden

Event Line

3 ■ Ehiogu (Foul)

15 ⊙ Job (Corner)

HALF TIME 1-0

63 ■ Davis S (Foul)

67 ⊙ Nemeth (Indirect Free Kick)

69 ⇄ Legwinski (Off) Hayles (On)

87 ■ Djetou (Foul)

90 ⊙ Hayles (Indirect Free Kick)

FULL TIME 2-1

Statistics

Middlesbrough			Fulham	
This Season	This Fixture		This Fixture	This Season
77	6	Shots On Target	5	98
105	9	Shots Off Target	3	107
2	0	Hit Woodwork	0	7
65	6	Caught Offside	3	45
79	9	Corners	1	77
281	15	Fouls	18	290
45%	58%	Possession	42%	44%

League Standings

Pos (pos before)		W	D	L	F	A	Pts
12 (15)	Middlesbro	6	6	7	16	19	24
7 (5)	Fulham	8	4	8	31	28	28

Premiership Milestone

75 The game marked Edwin van der Sar's 75th Premiership appearance.

a volley, but Knight made the block.

Then came a really bad miss by Gareth Southgate, as Downing delivered another telling cross, which the Boro captain somehow headed over from four yards out.

Juninho was the next Boro player to waste an opportunity, heading Szilard Nemeth's delicious chip straight at van der Sar.

The second half was also mostly Middlesbrough, though Malbranque showed we still had something left in the tank when he stepped neatly inside Downing's challenge and rolled a tempting ball across the penalty area, only for Luis Boa Morte to slice his shot wide.

The home side wasted another opportunity in the 54th minute when Downing picked out Franck Queudrue with a wicked free kick to the far post which he headed over an empty goal.

A Downing free kick indirectly led to Boro's second goal on 67 minutes.

After van der Sar dropped the ball under pressure, Ehiogu held off the Dutch keeper and nudged the ball to Southgate, who squared for Nemeth to side-foot home.

We managed a late consolation when Mills blocked Sean Davis' shot on the line and Barry Hayles rammed the loose ball home.

"One or two players have suffered a loss of confidence." Chris Coleman

Fulham 2
Everton 1

Match Details

Premiership
Saturday 10th January 2004
Venue: Loftus Road
Attendance: 17,103
Referee: G.Poll

Premiership Fixture History

Pl:3 Draws:0	Wins	⚽	■	■
Fulham	3	6	4	1
Everton	0	1	4	1

Starting Line-up

van der Sar

Djetou   Knight   Melville   Green

Clark (c)   Legwinski   S.Davis

Malbranque   Boa Morte

Saha

Jeffers   Campbell

Kilbane   Linderoth   Carsley   Radzinski

Naysmith   Unsworth   Weir (c)   Hibbert

Martyn

Petta, Crossley,   Rooney, McFadden,
Inamoto, Hayles,   Ferguson,Simonsen,
Sava.   Pistone.

Two Lees, Clark and Carsley, go for the ball

Goals from Louis Saha and Steed Malbranque helped to halt our slide down the Premiership table.

The two Frenchmen posed a constant threat to Everton, looking sharp around the penalty area and chasing every ball as we secured only our second league win in six outings.

We carved Everton open with barely a minute on the clock, Sean Davis concluding his run across midfield by passing to Malbranque, who weaved his way into the area before testing Nigel Martyn with a powerful drive.

Kevin Campbell made a mess of a fine opportunity at the other end before Everton threatened again in the seventh minute, Francis Jeffers crossing to the far post for Tomasz Radzinski, whose header was kept out by the sharp reactions of Edwin van der Sar.

After Martyn stopped a long-range effort from Davis, Everton went straight back on the attack, with Kevin Kilbane missing a sitter after some good work from Radzinski.

Jeffers failed to make the most of a good chance after doing all the hard work before we also wasted a good one, Saha nodding wide from close range.

The deadlock was broken just before the interval when Gary Naysmith brought down Malbranque as he raced in on goal. Referee Graham Poll immediately signalled for a penalty, which Saha tucked home.

We began the second half in the best possible way, as Everton's defence gave Malbranque time and space to unleash a perfectly-placed shot inches out of the reach of a despairing dive from Martyn and into the corner of the net.

Everton boss David Moyes introduced Wayne Rooney on 56 minutes in a bid to cut the deficit.

The England striker wasted no time in getting involved and saw a shot cleared off the line by Zat Knight. Van der Sar then stretched out a boot to keep out his goalbound header.

Luis Boa Morte was denied by some fine keeping at the other end, following his lightning run into the box.

Everton finally pulled one back, as Kilbane collected the ball in midfield, ran a few paces and then pulled the trigger from 30 yards out, lashing home a spectacular strike which arrived too late to salvage the match for the visitors.

"I'm delighted with the way the day has gone, and I think we deserved to win." Chris Coleman

Sylvain Legwinski tangles with David Unsworth

Event Line

45 ⊙ **Saha (Penalty)**

HALF TIME 1-0

46 ⊙ **Malbranque (Open Play)**

56 ⇄ Carsley (Off) Rooney (On)

57 ⇄ Campbell (Off) Ferguson (On)

57 ⇄ Radzinski (Off) McFadden (On)

81 ⊙ Kilbane (Open Play)

83 ⇄ **Boa Morte (Off) Petta (On)**

FULL TIME 2-1

Statistics

Fulham			Everton
This Season	This Fixture		This Fixture	This Season
108	10	Shots On Target	5	94
110	3	Shots Off Target	9	132
7	0	Hit Woodwork	0	6
46	1	Caught Offside	1	55
82	5	Corners	7	134
308	18	Fouls	10	268
44%	53%	Possession	47%	47%

League Standings

Pos (pos before)	W	D	L	F	A	Pts
6 (7) Fulham	9	4	8	33	29	31
12 (11) Everton	6	6	9	25	28	24

Premiership Milestone

100 Andy Melville made his 100th Premiership appearance.

Premiership Milestone

Fulham's Bobby Petta, on loan from Celtic, made his Premiership debut

Newcastle United 3
Fulham 1

A wonder strike from Laurent Robert capped an impressive Newcastle win, while we were left to contemplate life without Louis Saha.

The in-demand Frenchman was conspicuous by his absence, as he discussed a proposed move to Manchester United.

The home side were rarely stretched in the 4,000th league game in their history, and Sean Davis' 74th-minute strike proved scant consolation.

In Saha's absence, Barry Hayles was asked to lead the line, with Luis Boa Morte joining him whenever possible from wide on the left.

The Portuguese flier threatened at regular intervals during the early stages, his best effort a 19th-minute strike which hit the side netting from a narrow angle.

Newcastle defender Andy O'Brien got the ball rolling with just four minutes gone, slamming home a close-range shot after Jonathan Woodgate had recycled a Robert corner and Alan Shearer had seen his effort blocked.

On 18 minutes, Sylvain Legwinski was forced to limp off with

Match Details

Premiership
Monday 19th January 2004
Venue: St James' Park
Attendance: 50,104
Referee: N.S.Barry

Premiership Fixture History

	Pl:3	Draws:1	Wins ⚽	■	■
Newcastle United	2	6	1	0	
Fulham	0	2	3	1	

Starting Line-up

Given
Hughes   O'Brien   Woodgate   Bernard
Solano   Jenas   Speed   Robert
Dyer
Shearer (c)
Boa Morte   Hayles   Malbranque
S.Davis   Legwinski   Clark (c)
Bocanegra   Goma   Knight   Djetou
van der Sar

Viana, Ambrose, Ameobi, Harper, Bramble.

Volz, Crossley, Green, Sava, Petta.

Luis Boa Morte and Aaron Hughes in action

Carlos Bocanegra and Nolberto Solano

Event Line

4 ⚽ O'Brien (Corner)

18 🔄 Legwinski (Off) Volz (On)

41 ⚽ Speed (Corner)

HALF TIME 2-0

54 ⚽ Robert (Open Play)

66 🔄 Hayles (Off) Sava (On)

74 ⚽ Davis S (Open Play)

77 ▓ Djetou (Foul)

84 🔄 Robert (Off) Viana (On)

84 🔄 Shearer (Off) Ameobi (On)

84 🔄 Solano (Off) Ambrose (On)

FULL TIME 3-1

Statistics

Newcastle Utd			Fulham	
This Season	This Fixture		This Fixture	This Season
109	9	Shots On Target	6	114
122	1	Shots Off Target	7	117
6	0	Hit Woodwork	0	7
78	4	Caught Offside	1	47
145	7	Corners	4	86
286	14	Fouls	11	319
48%	52%	Possession	48%	44%

League Standings

Pos (pos before)	W	D	L	F	A	Pts
5 (7) Newcastle	8	9	5	30	23	33
7 (6) Fulham	9	4	9	34	32	31

Premiership Milestone

75 Alain Goma made his 75th Premiership appearance for Fulham, against his former club.

Premiership Milestone

Carlos Bocanegra, signed from Chicago Fire, made his Premiership debut.

a cut shin following a rugged challenge from Jermaine Jenas.

Gary Speed doubled his side's advantage four minutes before the interval, heading a Nolberto Solano corner past the stranded Edwin van der Sar at the near post.

Hayles did well to work himself a shooting opportunity just before the break, only to be denied by Olivier Bernard's sliding tackle.

We needed a quick second-half score if we were going to salvage anything from the game, but a sizeable helping of Gallic flair put paid to our hopes.

Robert picked up possession on the left and fed the ball inside to Speed. Jenas collected from the Welshman and slid the ball into the path of Solano, who floated in a cross which Robert, having sauntered into the middle, dispatched into the net with an outrageous overhead kick on 54 minutes.

We were finding it increasingly difficult to break through Newcastle's defence, while Robert, Solano and Kieron Dyer were starting to punch holes in our own rearguard with increasing regularity.

Still, the next goal would be ours, Davis driving in a low 25-yarder which went in off Shay Given's right-hand post with 16 minutes to go.

"I don't think the loss of Louis (Saha) will cause us a problem in terms of goals. We created some good chances, and we scored a goal as well." Lee Clark

Everton

Match Details

F.A. Cup Fourth Round
Sunday 25th January 2004
Venue: Goodison Park
Attendance: 27,862
Referee: D.J.Gallagher

Starting Line-up

Martyn

Hibbert   Stubbs (c)   Unsworth   Pistone

Rooney   Nyarko   Gravesen   Kilbane

Radzinski   Ferguson

Hayles

Boa Morte   Malbranque
Clark (c)   Djetou   S.Davis

Bocanegra   Goma   Knight   Volz

van der Sar

Naysmith, Jeffers,   Sava, Inamoto,
Campbell, Carsley,   Petta, Green,
Simonsen.   Crossley.

Barry Hayles takes on Wayne Rooney

Everton 1
Fulham 1

Everton striker Francis Jeffers netted in the final minute to keep the Toffees' F.A. Cup hopes alive.

The home side started brightly, Kevin Kilbane releasing Tomasz Radzinski, who cut inside Moritz Volz to fire a dipping 20-yarder just over the crossbar.

Duncan Ferguson went close on 14 minutes when he met a Kilbane cross and saw the effort turned off the line and over by Carlos Bocanegra.

Everton continued to press, Wayne Rooney and Alan Stubbs combining to set up Kilbane, but his shot didn't have enough power to trouble Edwin van der Sar.

Barry Hayles then emerged on the right of the box for a clear shooting chance which Nigel Martyn turned around a post with his legs.

Kilbane looked to have put his side ahead, but the goal was disallowed for handball.

Alessandro Pistone then lashed a shot into the side netting, while Sean Davis drilled a low shot just wide.

On 38 minutes, Kilbane saw a powerful goalbound header from Thomas Gravesen's corner hit Bocanegra a yard from the line.

Kilbane then wasted another good chance, shooting wide after Pistone and Rooney had set him up.

Everton's best plan of attack continued to be Radzinski down the left against Volz, but a flurry of crosses and corners at the start of the second half failed to give them the breakthrough.

That came at the other end on 49 minutes.

Steed Malbranque played in Volz, whose cross was palmed out to Bocanegra. The American's blocked shot then fell to Davis, who prodded past a stranded Martyn from six yards.

We went close to a second on 68 minutes, as Davis' control in the box left Hayles with a glittering opportunity, but he fired the ball into the side netting.

Rooney unsuccessfully claimed handball against Zat Knight in the box before van der Sar produced a fine reflex save to beat out Ferguson's angled drive.

Everton boss David Moyes introduced Jeffers for fullback Pistone on 85 minutes, a move which paid rich dividends five minutes later.

Gravesen's corner was met by Ferguson's head, and when the ball dropped into a packed six yard box after van der Sar's save, Jeffers forced it over the line.

"Everton kept going and Franny did what he does best. But we will go back to Loftus Road and look to kill them off."
Chris Coleman

Event Line

HALF TIME 0-0

49 ⊙ **Davis (Open Play)**

56 ▌ Rooney (Dissent)

58 ⇄ Unsworth (Off) Naysmith (On)

58 ▌ **Hayles (Foul)**

78 ▌ **Goma (Foul)**

81 ⇄ **Hayles (Off) Sava (On)**

85 ⇄ Pistone (Off) Jeffers (On)

90 ⊙ Jeffers (Corner)

90 ▌ **Malbranque (Foul)**

FULL TIME 1-1

Statistics

Everton		Fulham
11	Shots On Target	3
13	Shots Off Target	3
0	Hit Woodwork	0
4	Caught Offside	4
14	Corners	1
8	Fouls	14

Sean Davis celebrates scoring

Match Details

Premiership
Saturday 31st January 2004
Venue: Loftus Road
Attendance: 17,024
Referee: M.D.Messias

Premiership Fixture History

Pl:3 Draws:0	Wins ⚽	■	■
Fulham	2	5	3	0
Tottenham Hotspur 1	5	4	0

Starting Line-up

McBride, Petta, Crossley, Inamoto, Sava.

Zamora, Burch, Kelly, Bunjevcevic, Jackson.

Steed Malbranque scores from the penalty spot

Fulham 2
Tottenham Hotspur 1

Brian McBride marked his debut with the goal which ended Tottenham's 100% Premiership record in 2004.

The USA international, signed the previous week from Columbus Crew but familiar to English fans after a loan spell at Everton, came off the bench after 59 minutes and bundled home the winner just eight minutes later to seal our comeback.

The swirling wind and rain made good football hard to come by, but the game sprang to life on 16 minutes when keeper Edwin van der Sar needed every inch of his giant frame to dive to his right and tip Robbie Keane's fierce low drive onto his post.

Spurs won a penalty two minutes later, as Ian Pearce blocked the ball with his hand after Keane had tried to chip him.

Keane confidently tucked the ball into the bottom-left corner to register his ninth league goal of the season and his second from the spot in successive Premiership games.

We almost levelled three minutes later, Steed Malbranque playing in Barry Hayles, whose shot from the edge of the area was brilliantly saved by Kasey Keller.

We earned our own penalty in injury time.

Gary Doherty tried to clear down the right and Stephane Dalmat lost possession. Luis Boa Morte charged forward and was tripped by Michael Brown right on the penalty box line. The referee awarded the spot-kick and Malbranque fired the equaliser into the top-right corner.

Helder Postiga had two good chances to restore Spurs' advantage soon after the break, but he miskicked wildly from close range to squander the first and was then denied by van der Sar.

Chris Coleman introduced McBride in place of Hayles and he went close on 65 minutes, racing towards goal from wide on the right before attempting a lob which countryman Keller managed to block.

But we were celebrating just two minutes later – and it was McBride who got the final touch.

A Sean Davis corner on the left was headed down at the far post by Pearce. Keller did well to stop it, but McBride pounced on the line to knock the ball home.

"In the first half we got out of jail, because I didn't think we deserved to go in at 1-1. They coped better than us, but we upped it in the second half and got the result." Chris Coleman

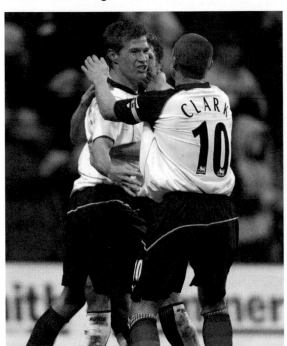

Brian McBride celebrates his goal

Event Line

18 ⚽ Keane (Penalty)

31 ▌ Ziege (Foul)

45 ⚽ **Malbranque (Penalty)**

HALF TIME 1-1

56 ▌ **Hayles (Foul)**

59 ⮀ **Hayles (Off) McBride (On)**

67 ⚽ **McBride (Corner)**

79 ⮀ Postiga (Off) Zamora (On)

89 ⮀ **Boa Morte (Off) Petta (On)**

FULL TIME 2-1

Statistics

Fulham			Tottenham	
This Season	This Fixture		This Fixture	This Season
124	10	Shots On Target	4	95
124	7	Shots Off Target	2	132
7	0	Hit Woodwork	0	5
48	1	Caught Offside	3	68
96	10	Corners	13	129
326	7	Fouls	13	377
45%	56%	Possession	44%	47%

League Standings

Pos (pos before)		W	D	L	F	A	Pts
7 (7)	Fulham	10	4	9	36	33	34
13 (11)	Tottenham	8	3	12	27	33	27

Premiership Milestone

Ian Pearce made his first Premiership appearance for Fulham.

Premiership Milestone

Brian McBride scored on his first Premiership appearance for Fulham.

January Review

Month in Numbers

Games Played: **6**
Games Won: **3**
Games Drawn: **1**
Games Lost: **2**
Goals For: **9**
Goals Against: **9**

Results this Month

FA Cup, 04/01/2004
Fulham 2-1 Cheltenham

Premiership, 07/01/2004
Middlesbro 2-1 Fulham

Premiership, 10/01/2004
Fulham 2-1 Everton

Premiership, 19/01/2004
Newcastle 3-1 Fulham

FA Cup, 25/01/2004
Everton 1-1 Fulham

Premiership, 31/01/2004
Fulham 2-1 Tottenham

Premiership Table

Pos	(Dec)		Pl	W	D	L	F	A	Diff	Pts
1	(1)	Man Utd	23	17	2	4	43	17	+26	53
2	(2)	Arsenal	22	15	7	0	42	14	+28	52
3	(3)	Chelsea	22	14	4	4	40	17	+23	46
4	(4)	Charlton	23	10	7	6	32	25	+7	37
5	(6)	Liverpool	23	9	7	7	32	24	+8	34
6	(7)	Newcastle	23	8	10	5	31	24	+7	34
7	**(5)**	**Fulham**	**23**	**10**	**4**	**9**	**36**	**33**	**+3**	**34**
8	(12)	Bolton	23	8	8	7	28	34	-6	32
9	(9)	Birmingham	22	8	7	7	20	26	-6	31
10	(8)	Southampton	23	8	6	9	23	21	+2	30
11	(10)	Aston Villa	23	8	6	9	26	27	-1	30
12	(15)	Middlesbro'	22	7	7	8	23	26	-3	28
13	(18)	Tottenham	23	8	3	12	27	33	-6	27
14	(11)	Everton	23	6	7	10	25	29	-4	25
15	(13)	Man City	22	5	8	9	31	33	-2	23
16	(14)	Blackburn	22	6	5	11	32	36	-4	23
17	(16)	Portsmouth	23	6	5	12	25	33	-8	23
18	(17)	Leicester	23	4	8	11	31	43	-12	20
19	(20)	Wolves	23	4	8	11	20	44	-24	20
20	(19)	Leeds	23	4	5	14	19	47	-28	17

Premiership Progression

Win: ■ Draw: ■ Loss: ■   League position: **8**   League position 2002-03: **8**   Home fixtures in black

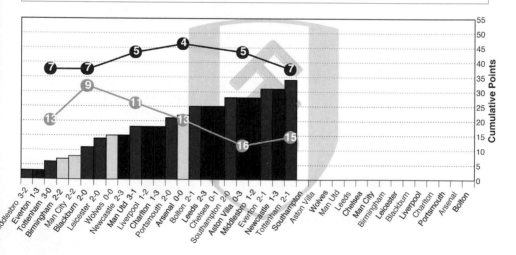

January Review

Premiership Performance

	Jan	03-04
Shots On Target	31	124
Shots Off Target	20	124
Hit Woodwork	0	7
Clean Sheets	0	7
Failed To Score	0	4
Caught Offside	6	48
Corners	20	96
Own Goals For	0	0
Own Goals Against	0	1

Goals Resulting From

	Jan		03-04	
	F	A	F	A
Open Play	2	2	28	20
Set Piece	4	5	8	12

How Goals Scored

	Jan		03-04	
	F	A	F	A
Right Foot	3	3	17	15
Left Foot	3	3	18	12
Header	0	1	1	5

When Goals Scored

	Jan		03-04	
	F	A	F	A
First Half	2	4	14	15
Second Half	4	3	22	17

Top Goal Scorers

	Jan	03-04
L. Saha	1	13
L. Boa Morte	0	5
S. Malbranque	2	4
B. Hayles	1	4
S. Davis	1	3

Top Goal Assists

	Jan	03-04
S. Malbranque	1	11
L. Saha	1	5
B. Hayles	0	3
L. Boa Morte	1	3
L. Clark	0	3

Player of the Month

Steed Malbranque

Goals: **2** Assists: **1**

While the loss of Louis Saha to Manchester United at the end of the month was a blow, most fans would have been delighted that it was he and not Malbranque who had departed. The playmaker continued to pull the strings, showing an eye for scoring goals as well as creating them. Having already won a penalty, a drive from distance proved decisive against Everton. Then, against Tottenham, Malbranque netted an equaliser from the spot, as the Cottagers came from behind to win.

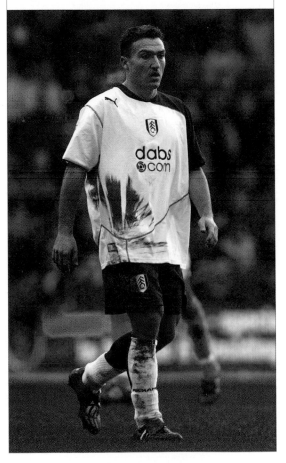

Fulham 2
Everton 1 (AET)

F.A. Cup Fourth Round replay
Wednesday 4th February 2004
Venue: Loftus Road
Attendance: 11,551
Referee: P.A.Durkin

Starting Line-up

van der Sar

Volz   Knight   Goma   Bocanegra

S.Davis   Djetou   Clark (c)
Malbranque   Boa Morte
Hayles

Radzinski   Rooney

Kilbane   Gravesen   Nyarko   Carsley

Naysmith   Unsworth   Pistone   Hibbert

Martyn

Petta, Sava,
Rehman, Green,
Crossley.

Watson, Jeffers,
Linderoth, Clarke,
Simonsen.

Fulham's Sean Davis beats Everton's Alex Nyarko

Steed Malbranque's extra-time winner led us past Everton and into a home tie against West Ham in the fifth round of the F.A. Cup.

Junichi Inamoto had opened the scoring by powering a 25-yard shot into the bottom corner on 57 minutes.

And the goal looked to be enough to secure us victory until Francis Jeffers struck in the dying seconds of normal time.

But Malbranque ensured penalties were not needed by netting from close range.

We were quickly into our stride, Malbranque rifling a shot across the Everton goal after two minutes.

Sean Davis also powered a shot off target before Everton were denied by the woodwork.

Tomasz Radzinski raced clear, only to see his angled shot come back off the post and into the grateful arms of keeper Edwin van der Sar.

We escaped again when Wayne Rooney failed to make proper contact with his header from six yards and allowed Carlos Bocanegra to head off the line.

Davis almost made Everton pay for the miss when he forced the in-form Nigel Martyn into a crucial one-handed save.

There were chances at either end to start the second half,

Alain Goma stretches for the ball.

Event Line

32 ■ Carsley (Foul)

HALF TIME 0-0

57 ⚽ Inamoto (Open Play)

62 ⇄ Nyarko (Off) Watson (On)

63 ⇄ Radzinski (Off) Jeffers (On)

81 ⇄ Hayles (Off) Sava (On)

90 ⚽ Jeffers (Open Play)

FULL TIME 1-1

91 ⇄ Inamoto (Off) Petta (On)

102 ⚽ Malbranque (Open Play)

AFTER EXTRA-TIME 2-1

Statistics

Fulham		Everton
13	Shots On Target	12
7	Shots Off Target	4
1	Hit Woodwork	1
0	Caught Offside	8
11	Corners	15
12	Fouls	20

Moritz Volz blocking Kevin Kilbane's shot at full stretch, while Zat Knight headed just over.

Inamoto then broke the deadlock, as good work from Luis Boa Morte gave the Japanese midfielder time and space to bury a 25-yard shot into the bottom corner.

Malbranque wasted a chance to extend our lead before Everton's pressure was rewarded with a late goal.

Jeffers, who had rescued Everton in the first game at Goodison Park, once again played the role of tormentor, rising to glance a header past the despairing van der Sar after Lee Carsley had nodded the ball towards the penalty spot.

Jeffers had two gilt-edged chances in an enthralling finish, but he missed with a header from point-blank range and then fired over just before the game went into extra time.

The opportunities kept coming for Jeffers, but he somehow scooped a shot over from close in, before a well-worked move ended with Malbranque powering in a shot from eight yards.

"We were a bit stunned by the goal and feeling very tired, but Cookie was fantastic. He went round talking to everyone and really got us going again. He gave us the confidence to think that we could go out there and beat them again." Martin Djetou

Match Details

Premiership
Saturday 7th February 2004
Venue: St Mary's Stadium
Attendance: 31,820
Referee: A.P.D'Urso

Premiership Fixture History

Pl:3 Draws:2	Wins	⚽		
Southampton	1	5	3	0
Fulham	**0**	**3**	**4**	**0**

Starting Line-up

Niemi
Dodd (c) M.Svensson Higginbotham Le Saux
Telfer A.Svensson Delap Pahars
Phillips Ormerod
McBride
Boa Morte Malbranque
Clark (c) Djetou S.Davis
Bocanegra Pearce Knight Volz
van der Sar

Beattie, Smith,
Baird, Hall,
Fernandes.

Petta, Legwinski,
Inamoto, Crossley,
Hayles.

Ian Pearce and Anders Svensson

Southampton 0
Fulham 0

Edwin van der Sar's acrobatics kept Southampton at bay at St Mary's.

The big shot-stopper was on top form, making superb saves off Brett Ormerod – twice – and Anders Svensson.

The home side dominated the opening exchanges, Graeme Le Saux drilling in a right-footed shot from 20 yards which flashed wide of the post after four minutes.

Kevin Phillips looked lively for Southampton, but was largely starved of possession.

Saints almost scored a cracking goal at the midway point of the half.

Phillips swung over an arching cross from the right to Ormerod, who stretched out his left boot to volley goalwards. But van der Sar was equal to it, making a brilliant save to tip the ball over.

Van der Sar saved us again five minutes before the break when Ian Pearce made a hash of a clearance.

Anders Svensson nipped in and hammered a shot, but the big Dutch keeper pulled off a great parry.

A moment of magic from Ormerod almost broke the deadlock 30 seconds after the interval.

The frontman slipped in-between Pearce and Carlos Bocanegra on the right flank before cutting inside and rifling a shot which van der Sar diverted past the near post with a leg.

The hosts went even closer to the opener after 56 minutes.

Centre-back Michael Svensson headed a right-wing corner goalwards and Moritz Volz blocked and then cleared as Ormerod prepared to smash home the rebound.

Referee Andy D'Urso waved away Saints' penalty appeals when Le Saux's pull-back appeared to hit Pearce's arm.

We finally had our first attempt on goal in the 68th minute when Brian McBride collected Sean Davis' excellent pull-back and thumped a 10-yard shot into Danny Higginbotham's midriff.

Marian Pahars had a golden chance 17 minutes from time, but he fired his far-post shot against van der Sar's body.

Antti Niemi made his first save with 11 minutes to play, diving low to his right to grab Davis' 20-yard effort.

We were coming more into the game, and the Finnish shot-stopper had to be alert to keep things level, making a good save to deny McBride's close-range effort.

**"I didn't tell them to go out and defend for 90 minutes. It's not negative tactics when you've got 35 points and are seventh in the League."
Chris Coleman**

Zat Knight is challenged by Brett Ormerod

Event Line

| 31 | ▊ | Malbranque (Foul) |

HALF TIME 0-0

58	⇄	**Malbranque (Off) Petta (On)**
65	⇄	**Clark (Off) Legwinski (On)**
70	▊	**Volz (Foul)**
74	▊	Phillips (Dissent)
75	⇄	Ormerod (Off) Beattie (On)
89	⇄	**Davis S (Off) Inamoto (On)**

FULL TIME 0-0

Statistics

| Southampton | | | **Fulham** | |
This Season	This Fixture		This Fixture	This Season
109	5	Shots On Target	2	126
138	7	Shots Off Target	3	127
8	0	Hit Woodwork	0	7
66	2	Caught Offside	1	49
150	17	Corners	3	99
328	12	Fouls	18	344
46%	55%	Possession	45%	45%

League Standings

Pos (pos before)	W	D	L	F	A	Pts
10 (10) Soton	8	7	9	23	21	31
7 (7) Fulham	10	5	9	36	33	35

Premiership Milestone

50 Zat Knight reached his half-century of Premiership appearances.

Fulham 1
Aston Villa 2

Match Details

Premiership
Wednesday 11th February 2004
Venue: Loftus Road
Attendance: 16,153
Referee: B.Knight

Premiership Fixture History

	Pl:3 Draws:1	Wins ⚽	◼	◼
Fulham	1	3	4	1
Aston Villa	1	3	6	0

Starting Line-up

van der Sar
Volz Knight Pearce Bocanegra
Clark (c) Djetou S.Davis
Malbranque Boa Morte
McBride

Angel Vassell
Barry Hitzlsperger Hendrie Solano
Samuel Johnsen Mellberg (c) Delaney
Sorensen

Petta, Hayles, Crossley, Legwinski, Inamoto.

De la Cruz, Postma, Whittingham, Ridgewell, Crouch.

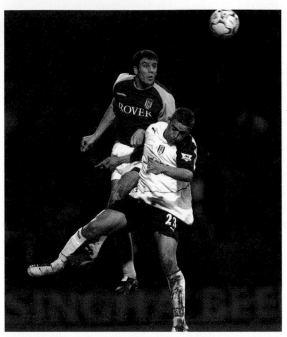

Sean Davis and Mark Delaney take to the air.

Villa capitalised on some poor defending to come back from conceding an early goal and grab the points at Loftus Road.

Luis Boa Morte put us ahead after just 52 seconds when he slammed home Lee Clark's pass from an angle.

Juan Pablo Angel then equalised after Edwin van der Sar had parried his initial header, before Darius Vassell was left unmarked to head the second at a corner.

We had the perfect start with Boa Morte's goal, but it was all downhill from there and van der Sar had to take the blame for the equaliser. Angel got on the end of Thomas Hitzlsperger's free kick at the far post to poke a shot goalwards. Van der Sar should have easily snapped it up, but he could only parry the ball back to Angel, who made no mistake with the rebound.

Lee Hendrie's fine curling effort on 32 minutes forced van der Sar into a plunging save - tipping the ball round the post at full stretch. From the resulting corner, Vassell rose unmarked at the near post to head home Hitzlsperger's delivery.

We responded before the interval, with Villa keeper Thomas

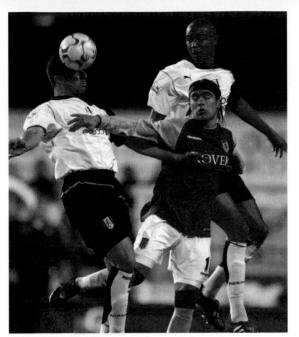

Zat Knight and Ian Pearce surround Juan Pablo Angel

Event Line

1 ⚽ **Boa Morte (Open Play)**

13 ⚽ Angel (Indirect Free Kick)

32 ⚽ Vassell (Corner)

HALF TIME 1-2

46 🔄 **Clark (Off) Petta (On)**

56 ■ **Davis S (Foul)**

58 ■ **Knight (Foul)**

70 🔄 **Djetou (Off) Hayles (On)**

75 ■ **Bocanegra (Foul)**

77 🔄 Delaney (Off) De la Cruz (On)

80 ■ Barry (Foul)

80 🔄 Barry (Off) Whittingham (On)

89 🔄 Hendrie (Off) Ridgewell (On)

FULL TIME 1-2

Sorensen making a great one-handed parry off Boa Morte's shot.

And on the stroke of half-time, Sorensen blocked Sean Davis' flick from Boa Morte's cross.

We started the second half as we'd ended the first – attacking Villa. Davis was in with a sight of goal, but snatched at his shot. Olof Mellberg, whose mistake had let Boa Morte in for the opener, then had a lucky escape, as he allowed Steed Malbranque to race on goal before the Frenchman was penalised for handball.

The game turned ugly two minutes later when Carlos Bocanegra was sent off for an aggressive two-footed lunge on Villa defender Mark Delaney.

The incident incensed Villa boss David O'Leary and sparked a melee between both benches, with the end result being that Delaney couldn't carry on and had to be replaced by Ulises De la Cruz.

Brian McBride almost grabbed an equaliser at the death with a volley off Barry Hayles' cross, but it bounced into the ground and off the crossbar.

"It was a great start. I thought it was a great goal by Boa, but after that we just took our foot off the gas."
Chris Coleman

Statistics

Fulham			Aston Villa	
This Season	This Fixture		This Fixture	This Season
131	5	Shots On Target	7	111
133	6	Shots Off Target	4	155
8	1	Hit Woodwork	0	8
49	0	Caught Offside	3	105
105	6	Corners	5	152
363	19	Fouls	19	393
45%	52%	Possession	48%	45%

League Standings

Pos (pos before)	W	D	L	F	A	Pts
8 (7) Fulham	10	5	10	37	35	35
7 (9) Aston Villa	10	6	9	30	28	36

Fulham 0
West Ham United 0

F.A. Cup Fifth Round
Saturday 14th February 2004
Venue: Loftus Road
Attendance: 14,705
Referee: G.Poll

Starting Line-up

van der Sar

Volz　　Knight　　Goma　　Bocanegra

S.Davis　Legwinski (c)

Malbranque　　　　　　Boa Morte

McBride　　Hayles

Connolly　　Deane

Etherington　Horlock　Carrick　Harewood

Ferdinand　Mullins　Dailly (c)　Repka

Bywater

Petta, Inamoto,
Djetou, Green,
Crossley.

Lomas, Mellor,
Quinn, Carole,
Shaaban.

Both sides had plenty of chances to seize a place in the last eight, but were denied by a combination of brilliant goalkeeping and occasionally wayward finishing at Loftus Road.

Sven-Goran Eriksson was in attendance, as he prepared for his England squad announcement for the friendly against Portugal.

He witnessed another lively performance by Luis Boa Morte, who would represent the hosts in the midweek match against England in Faro.

West Ham could have gone ahead after just 10 seconds, but Edwin van der Sar pulled off a great parry from Marlon Harewood's thumping volley.

We then hit back, with Steed Malbranque twice testing Hammers keeper Stephen Bywater.

Moritz Volz and Alain Goma both had shots at goal before Michael Carrick sent a fierce drive rising just over the angle of post and bar.

Zat Knight goes in bravely against Marlon Harewood.

Brian McBride and West Ham's Anton Ferdinand in action.

Event Line

HALF TIME 0-0

56 ⚽ **Boa Morte (Off) Petta (On)**

79 ⚽ Deane (Off) Mellor (On)

81 ▊ **Hayles (Foul)**

84 ▊ Connolly (Foul)

89 ⚽ Connolly (Off) Lomas (On)

90 ▊ **Bocanegra (Foul)**

FULL TIME 0-0

Statistics

Fulham		West Ham
6	Shots On Target	9
7	Shots Off Target	3
1	Hit Woodwork	0
4	Caught Offside	2
9	Corners	7
7	Fouls	6

We almost took the lead in bizarre fashion on 27 minutes.

Left-back Carlos Bocanegra, sent off for a wild two-footed lunge on Mark Delaney in the 2-1 defeat at home to Aston Villa, advanced into the box and mis-hit a cross-shot which looped against the far post.

Van der Sar twice denied the visitors as the interval approached, first blocking David Connolly's effort from an acute angle and then flinging his giant frame to his right to make a brilliant save off a thumping Brian Deane header.

The Hammers started strongly after the break, van der Sar clawing Matthew Etherington's awkward cross only as far as Deane, who blazed the loose ball over the top.

The visitors had a lucky escape after Tomas Repka and Christian Dailly sandwiched Barry Hayles right on the edge of the box, referee Graham Poll waving away our penalty appeals.

While West Ham were enjoying the better of the second half action, we were still looking a threat on the counter, Sean Davis testing Bywater with a looping header which he seized under his crossbar.

Dailly came up for a West Ham corner, but powered his header into the side netting.

Van der Sar then brilliantly pushed away a cross destined for Connolly's head before bravely throwing himself in front of Carrick's follow-up.

At the other end, Volz flashed an 18-yard strike just over before Bywater saved from Sylvain Legwinski as full-time neared.

**"Without van der Sar – who had a terrific game – we would be out of the FA Cup, and I wouldn't have had any complaints."
Chris Coleman**

Match Details

Premiership
Saturday 21st February 2004
Venue: Molineux
Attendance: 28,424
Referee: H.M.Webb

Premiership Fixture History

	Pl:1 Draws:0	Wins ⚽	■	■
Wolves	1	2	1	0
Fulham	**0**	**1**	**0**	**0**

Starting Line-up

Jones

Clyde Craddock Butler Naylor

Camara Ince (c) Rae Kennedy

Miller Cort

McBride Hayles

Boa Morte Legwinski S.Davis Malbranque

Bocanegra Pearce Knight Volz

van der Sar (c)

Ganea, Cameron, Oakes, Luzhny, Iversen.

Petta, Djetou, Crossley, Green, Inamoto.

Steed Malbranque under pressure from Alex Rae

Wolves 2
Fulham 1

Goals from Paul Ince and Carl Cort helped Wolves to a win that saw them climb off the bottom of the table.

The sides were evenly matched in the early stages, but Wolves increasingly asserted themselves as the game progressed.

Alex Rae embarked on a jinking run on seven minutes, but his low shot was well held by Edwin van der Sar.

Wolves turned their pressure into a goal on 20 minutes, Ince firing Rae's knock-down into the right-hand corner.

The home side almost doubled their advantage minutes later when a quickly taken free kick found Mark Kennedy, who drove just wide.

Ian Pearce almost grabbed an equaliser, stealing to the far post following a Sean Davis free kick, only to poke his shot into the side netting.

Kenny Miller then saw a shot saved by van der Sar after a neat chest-down from Carl Cort.

At the other end, Paul Jones tipped Brian McBride's volley off Luis Boa Morte's cross round the post.

Wolves extended their lead six minutes after the break when

Zat Knight keeps Carl Cort on his toes

Event Line

17 ■ Ince (Foul)

20 ⊙ Ince (Open Play)

HALF TIME 1-0

51 ⊙ Cort (Open Play)

67 ⮂ **Hayles (Off) Petta (On)**

74 ⮂ **Knight (Off) Djetou (On)**

78 ⮂ Miller (Off) Ganea (On)

84 ⊙ **Malbranque (Open Play)**

90 ⮂ Cort (Off) Cameron (On)

FULL TIME 2-1

Statistics

Wolves			Fulham	
This Season	This Fixture		This Fixture	This Season
101	7	Shots On Target	6	137
169	6	Shots Off Target	8	141
8	1	Hit Woodwork	0	8
55	1	Caught Offside	3	52
122	8	Corners	6	111
380	16	Fouls	17	380
45%	44%	Possession	56%	46%

League Standings

Pos (pos before)	W	D	L	F	A	Pts
18 (20) Wolves	5	8	13	24	52	23
8 (8) Fulham	10	5	11	38	37	35

Premiership Milestone

100 Steed Malbranque made his 100th appearance in the Premiership.

a fortunate ricochet outside our area fell to Cort, who was left with the simple task of poking the ball home.

Ince teed up Mark Clyde on 66 minutes, but the youngster drove straight at van der Sar.

An Ince rocket then cannoned off the underside of the bar, with Cort's follow-up header claimed on the line by van der Sar.

We responded with a Sylvain Legwinski shot from range which fizzed just wide of Jones' right-hand post.

Cort then almost claimed his second, chesting down in the box before spooning his effort over the bar.

Steed Malbranque made it a tense last few minutes when he grabbed an 84th-minute goal.

Boa Morte's shot on the run was well saved by Jones, but Malbranque was on hand to tuck in the rebound.

We threw everyone forward in the search for an equaliser, but a suspect Wolves backline somehow survived.

The defeat left us looking for our first win on our travels since victory at Old Trafford back in October.

"The most disappointing thing for me is the way that we're losing games. We played with a fear of losing at the start of the season because we wanted to prove people wrong. The season could quite easily fizzle out unless we get that fear back into our game.
Chris Coleman

Match Details

F.A. Cup Fifth Round replay
Tuesday 24th February 2004
Venue: Upton Park
Attendance: 27,934
Referee: M.A.Riley

Starting Line-up

Bywater
Ferdinand Mullins Dailly (c) Quinn
Harewood Horlock Carrick Etherington
Deane Connolly

Boa Morte McBride
Petta Legwinski S.Davis Malbranque
Bocanegra Goma Djetou Volz
van der Sar

Mellor, Lee, Lomas, Carole, Ford.

Knight, Hayles, Inamoto, Crossley, McBribe.

Sylvain Legwinski takes on David Connolly

West Ham United 0
Fulham 3

Goals from Brian McBride, Barry Hayles and Luis Boa Morte booked us a place at Manchester United in the F.A. Cup Quarter-Finals.

Chris Coleman was absent with a virus, but two goals in the space of three second-half minutes before Boa Morte's 90th minute clincher must have aided his recovery.

Edwin van der Sar was the hero and he had to be alert early on with Kevin Horlock testing his handling from distance.

Marlon Harewood was the next to go close, just missing the foot of the upright with the Dutchman stranded out of position.

But van der Sar then pulled off a fantastic save to tip Harewood's vicious shot over the crossbar in the 20th minute.

David Connolly headed Matthew Etherington's free kick high and wide before Harewood was denied again when we got enough bodies in the way at a Michael Carrick corner.

It wasn't until the 27th minute that we got a meaningful shot on goal, Moritz Volz forcing Stephen Bywater into a fine save.

Boa Morte was guilty of a glaring miss when he put a free header off Bobby Petta's cross wide on 42 minutes.

Suddenly the match was flowing from end to end, with

Brian McBride is challenged by West Ham's Michael Carrick

Event Line

28 ▓ Mullins (Foul)

33 ▓ Horlock (Foul)

HALF TIME 0-0

48 ⇄ Djetou (Off) Knight (On)

73 ⇄ Deane (Off) Lomas (On)

73 ⇄ Petta (Off) Hayles (On)

76 ⊙ McBride (Open Play)

79 ⊙ Hayles (Open Play)

79 ⇄ Horlock (Off) Lee (On)

90 ⊙ Boa Morte (Open Play)

FULL TIME 0-3

Statistics

West Ham		Fulham
5	Shots On Target	8
3	Shots Off Target	3
0	Hit Woodwork	0
5	Caught Offside	2
6	Corners	3
10	Fouls	10

Bywater sprinting out to clear at the feet of Boa Morte before a stretching Harewood missed the target with a toe poke as the half drew to a close.

Steed Malbranque was the next to go close, dragging an 18-yarder wide of the far post.

Zat Knight should have done better with his header after Carlos Bocanegra nodded Sean Davis' corner back to him.

Davis then shot marginally wide before Bywater was forced to save from McBride.

The warning signs were there, and we were soon ahead. Bocanegra's deft chip sailed over the head of Hayden Mullins and McBride controlled with his chest before firing into the top corner.

Van der Sar then denied Harewood before Hayles made it two with a close-range tap-in 11 minutes from time.

Boa Morte added a third at the end, despite Anton Ferdinand's attempt to clear off the line.

"It's a big game for us and the possibility of going to Old Trafford for the Quarter Final should be enough of an incentive for any player. We're at the stage of the season where we're not realistically going to get sucked into a relegation battle."
Chris Coleman

Fulham 1
Manchester United 1

We put yet another dent into Manchester United's title aspirations with a 1-1 draw at Loftus Road.

Louis Saha fired the visitors ahead against his old side before Luis Boa Morte, who had come to the fore since Saha's departure, made United pay for not capitalising on their first half dominance by hitting the equaliser after 64 minutes.

Saha almost made the most sensational of starts after just nine seconds, racing onto Diego Forlan's angled pass and firing goalwards from 14 yards. The ball beat Edwin van der Sar, but skidded just beyond the far post.

But the Frenchman wouldn't have to wait long to stamp his mark on the game.

Roy Carroll flung the ball out to Cristiano Ronaldo, who slipped it inside for Saha to race into the area and fire past van der Sar on 14 minutes.

United went close to a second, as Darren Fletcher robbed Alain Goma and curled a shot a yard wide.

We went agonisingly close to equalising on 28 minutes, Sylvain Legwinski meeting Sean Davis' left-wing corner with a

Match Details

Premiership
Saturday 28th February 2004
Venue: Loftus Road
Attendance: 18,306
Referee: A.G.Wiley

Premiership Fixture History

	Pl:3	Draws:2	Wins ⊙	▪	▪
Fulham	0	4	2	0	
Manchester United	1	5	8	0	

Starting Line-up

van der Sar
Volz — Pearce — Goma — Green
Malbranque — S.Davis — Legwinski (c) — Petta
McBride — Boa Morte
Saha — Forlan
Ronaldo — P.Neville — Scholes — Fletcher
Fortune — Brown — Keane (c) — O'Shea
Carroll

Pembridge, Inamoto, Crossley, Knight Rehman.
Giggs, Howard, van Nistelrooy, Djemba-Djemba, Bellion.

United's Darren Fletcher is chased by Fulham's Adam Green

Luis Boa Morte scores

Event Line

14 ⚽ Saha (Open Play)

42 ◼ Davis S (Foul)

45 ◼ Brown (Foul)

HALF TIME 0-1

55 ◼ Forlan (Ung Conduct)

64 ⚽ Boa Morte (Open Play)

66 ⇄ Petta (Off) Pembridge (On)

69 ◼ van Nistelrooy (Ung Conduct)

72 ⇄ Fletcher (Off) Giggs (On)

72 ⇄ Forlan (Off) van Nistelrooy (On)

80 ⇄ Malbranque (Off) Inamoto (On)

FULL TIME 1-1

Statistics

Fulham			Man Utd	
This Season	This Fixture		This Fixture	This Season
139	2	Shots On Target	8	148
147	6	Shots Off Target	7	164
8	0	Hit Woodwork	0	9
56	4	Caught Offside	6	106
115	4	Corners	3	144
396	16	Fouls	20	314
46%	49%	Possession	51%	53%

League Standings

Pos (pos before)		W	D	L	F	A	Pts
8 (9)	Fulham	10	6	11	39	38	36
3 (2)	Man Utd	18	4	5	51	25	58

header which flicked to safety off Roy Keane.

United started the second half in identical fashion to the first, only this time it was Ronaldo who fired just beyond the far post.

We then stunned the visitors by grabbing an equaliser on 64 minutes, Steed Malbranque slipping a pass through to Boa Morte, who spun Wes Brown and fired through Carroll's legs.

Referee Alan Wiley denied United the opportunity to retake an immediate lead when he turned down what looked a fair penalty claim.

Saha charged onto Forlan's through-ball and clipped it beyond van der Sar, who stuck out his arm and sent the striker tumbling to the ground.

After dismissing their appeal, Wiley further enraged United by booking Ruud van Nistelrooy for complaining while he was still warming up on the touchline.

Van Nistelrooy made a terrible hash of a golden chance with four minutes left.

Fellow sub Ryan Giggs chipped a pass into him, but he bundled into his countryman van der Sar and the ball bobbled wide.

**"Boa gives everything. He's got that enthusiasm, that electric pace. He certainly had a few occasions where he looked like he was causing them all sorts of problems."
Fulham Assistant Manager Steve Kean**

February Review

Month in Numbers

Games Played: **7**
Games Won: **2**
Games Drawn: **3**
Games Lost: **2**
Goals For: **8**
Goals Against: **6**

Results this Month

FA Cup, 04/02/2004
Fulham 2-1 Everton
Premiership, 07/02/2004
Southampton 0-0 Fulham
Premiership, 11/02/2004
Fulham 1-2 Aston Villa
FA Cup, 14/02/2004
Fulham 0-0 West Ham
Premiership, 21/02/2004
Wolves 2-1 Fulham
FA Cup, 24/02/2004
West Ham 0-3 Fulham
Premiership, 28/02/2004
Fulham 1-1 Man Utd

Premiership Table

Pos	(Jan)		Pl	W	D	L	F	A	Diff	Pts
1	(2)	Arsenal	27	20	7	0	53	18	+35	67
2	(3)	Chelsea	27	18	4	5	48	21	+27	58
3	(1)	Man Utd	27	18	4	5	51	25	+26	58
4	(6)	Newcastle	27	10	12	5	38	28	+10	42
5	(4)	Charlton	27	11	7	9	38	34	+4	40
6	(5)	Liverpool	26	10	9	7	38	29	+9	39
7	(11)	Aston Villa	27	10	7	10	32	32	0	37
8	**(7)**	**Fulham**	**27**	**10**	**6**	**11**	**39**	**38**	**+1**	**36**
9	(9)	Birmingham	25	9	9	7	25	28	-3	36
10	(13)	Tottenham	26	10	4	12	39	42	-3	34
11	(8)	Bolton	26	8	10	8	32	40	-8	34
12	(10)	Southampton	27	8	9	10	27	27	0	33
13	(12)	Middlesbro'	25	8	7	10	27	31	-4	31
14	(14)	Everton	27	7	8	12	33	39	-6	29
15	(16)	Blackburn	27	7	7	13	39	44	-5	28
16	(15)	Man City	27	6	9	12	36	39	-3	27
17	(17)	Portsmouth	26	6	6	14	29	40	-11	24
18	(19)	Wolves	27	5	9	13	24	52	-28	24
19	(18)	Leicester	27	4	11	12	37	51	-14	23
20	(20)	Leeds	27	5	7	15	26	53	-27	22

Premiership Progression

Win:■ Draw:▨ Loss:■ League position: **8** League position 2002-03: 8 Home fixtures in black

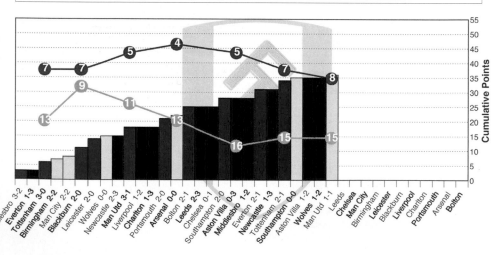

February Review

Premiership Performance

	Feb	03-04
Shots On Target	15	139
Shots Off Target	23	147
Hit Woodwork	1	8
Clean Sheets	1	8
Failed To Score	1	5
Caught Offside	8	56
Corners	19	115
Own Goals For	0	0
Own Goals Against	0	1

Goals Resulting From

	Feb		03-04	
	F	A	F	A
Open Play	3	3	31	23
Set Piece	0	2	8	14

How Goals Scored

	Feb		03-04	
	F	A	F	A
Right Foot	1	3	18	18
Left Foot	2	1	20	13
Header	0	1	1	6

When Goals Scored

	Feb		03-04	
	F	A	F	A
First Half	1	4	15	19
Second Half	2	1	24	18

Top Goal Scorers

	Feb	03-04
L. Saha	0	13
L. Boa Morte	2	7
S. Malbranque	1	5
B. Hayles	0	4
S. Davis	0	3

Top Goal Assists

	Feb	03-04
S. Malbranque	0	11
L. Saha	0	5
L. Boa Morte	1	4
L. Clark	1	4
B. Hayles	0	3

Player of the Month

Luis Boa Morte

Goals: **2** Assists: **1**

A winless month in the league provided few highlights, the exception being the form of Luis Boa Morte. The former Southampton man played a part in all four of Fulham's league goals. A strike against Aston Villa and an assist against Wolves counted for little. However, Boa Morte's equaliser at home to Manchester United did net Fulham a share of the spoils. The winger also featured in Portugal's friendly with England, and netted a late third in an F.A.Cup 5th Round Replay win at West Ham.

Match Details

F.A. Cup Quarter-Final
Saturday 6th March 2004
Venue: Old Trafford
Attendance: 67,614
Referee: R.Styles

Starting Line-up

Howard

P.Neville   Keane (c)   Brown   O'Shea

Ronaldo   Fletcher   Butt   Giggs

Scholes
van Nistelrooy

McBride
Boa Morte
Malbranque

Clark (c)   Legwinski   S.Davis

Green   Goma   Knight   Volz

van der Sar

Djemba-Djemba,   Pembridge, Petta,
Solskjaer, Carroll,   Hayles, Djetou,
Kleberson, Forlan.   Crossley.

Moritz Volz shields the ball from Ruud van Nistelrooy.

Manchester United 2
Fulham 1

Ruud van Nistelrooy's second successive F.A. Cup double saw Manchester United advance to the Semi-Finals for the first time since 1999.

Steed Malbranque's first half spot kick had put us in front before the flying Dutchman – whose goals had sent Manchester City spinning out of the competition in the previous round – smashed home close-range efforts either side of the interval.

Ryan Giggs had a chance to put the hosts ahead inside the first minute, but Alain Goma blocked his shot from Cristiano Ronaldo's cross.

Brian McBride then robbed Roy Keane and pushed a pass into the box intended for Luis Boa Morte.

Wes Brown looked favourite to get there first, but inexplicably the England international missed the ball completely and succeeded only in wiping out Boa Morte.

Referee Rob Styles had no choice but to award a 23rd minute spot-kick, which Malbranque slotted home with clinical efficiency.

It was the first penalty United had conceded on home soil in domestic combat for 11 years.

Two minutes later and United were level, van Nistelrooy crashing home on the half-volley off Giggs' precise low cross.

Zat Knight went close to a spectacular first goal as a Fulham player when his dipping shot from fully 30 yards bounced back off the crossbar on 34 minutes.

United's response sparked a fierce scramble in our penalty area, with van Nistelrooy and Giggs both having shots charged down.

The chances continued to flow at both ends, with Keane and van Nistelrooy failing by inches to make contact with Giggs' vicious free kick.

United's defence failed to cope with a set-piece and in the resulting scramble Sylvain Legwinski's first effort was blocked before he fired his second straight at Tim Howard.

We had a let-off on 55 minutes when Moritz Volz blocked Darren Fletcher off the ball and Ronaldo smacked the resulting free kick against the bar.

United stepped up a gear in search of a second goal and found it on 62 minutes.

Ronaldo collected from Fletcher on the right and steadied himself before producing the perfect service for van Nistelrooy to fire the winner from inside the six yard box.

"The attitude and commitment was all there. The difference between the sides was in the final third, they had a little bit more penetration than us." Steve Kean

Event Line

23 ⊙ **Malbranque (Penalty)**
25 ⊙ van Nistelrooy (Open Play)
30 ■ Keane (Foul)
45 ■ P.Neville (Foul)
HALF TIME 1-1
55 ■ **Volz (Foul)**
58 ■ **Boa Morte (Foul)**
62 ⊙ van Nistelrooy (Open Play)
63 ⮂ **McBride (Off) Hayles (On)**
64 ⮂ **Legwinski (Off) Pembridge (On)**
75 ⮂ Keane (Off) Djemba-Djemba (On)
81 ⮂ **Clark (Off) Petta (On)**
88 ⮂ Ronaldo (Off) Solskjaer (On)
90 ■ **Goma (Foul)**
90 ■ **Hayles (Foul)**
FULL TIME 2-1

Statistics

Man Utd		Fulham
9	Shots On Target	6
3	Shots Off Target	4
1	Hit Woodwork	1
4	Caught Offside	0
4	Corners	2
12	Fouls	17

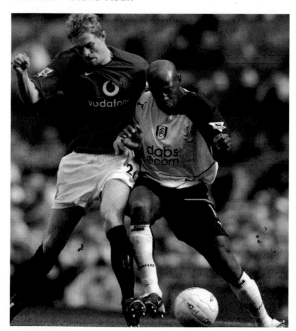

Luis Boa Morte against United's Darren Fletcher.

Fulham 2
Leeds United 0

Match Details

Premiership
Saturday 13th March 2004
Venue: Loftus Road
Attendance: 17,104
Referee: S.W.Dunn

Premiership Fixture History

Pl:3 Draws:1	Wins ⚽	■	■
Fulham	2	3	8	0
Leeds United	0	0	9	0

Starting Line-up

van der Sar

Volz — Knight — Pearce — Green

Malbranque — S.Davis — Legwinski (c) — Pembridge

Hayles — Boa Morte

Viduka — Smith

Milner — Seth — McPhail — Pennant

Domi — Matteo (c) — Caldwell — Kelly

Robinson

🧤 McBride, Crossley, Djetou, Inamoto, Petta.
🧤 Simon, Johnson, Carson, Harte, Richardson, Olembe.

Mark Pembridge surges past Jermaine Pennant.

We won for the first time in six weeks on the back of goals from Sean Davis and Luis Boa Morte.

Chris Coleman carried through with his threat to axe his misfiring stars, dropping Alain Goma and Brian McBride after their poor performances in the FA Cup Quarter-Final defeat at Manchester United. Ian Pearce and Barry Hayles were restored to the starting XI.

Our first clear chance came halfway through the opening period, Hayles making a nuisance of himself in the box before passing to Boa Morte, who hooked an awkward shot over the top.

At the other end, Pearce was in the right place at the right time to block Alan Smith's shot after his powerful surge into the box.

Boa Morte had another good chance four minutes before the break, as he raced onto Sylvain Legwinski's long ball upfield, only to scuff a weak shot straight at Paul Robinson.

Eddie Gray's basement dwellers almost grabbed a freak opener early in the second half, but Didier Domi's bouncing volley off Jermaine Pennant's far-post corner was clawed away by Edwin van der Sar.

We went close ourselves in the 50th minute, Robinson bravely saving twice in quick succession to deny Mark Pembridge. Robinson was left completely exposed four minutes later, but the unmarked Hayles headed Pembridge's corner wide. Boa Morte wasted another good chance, losing possession when in an excellent shooting position 12 yards out. Steed Malbranque was the next guilty party, as he dragged a shot harmlessly wide. But Davis made up for the misses with a classy opening goal after 71 minutes.

The midfielder played a neat one-two with Malbranque before smacking a 16-yarder into the bottom-left corner. We doubled our lead seven minutes from time when the Leeds defence went AWOL.

Pembridge returned a half-cleared free kick into the danger zone and Zat Knight crossed for Boa Morte to nod home.

Leeds wasted late chances to score, Seth Johnson shooting straight at van der Sar before Simon Johnson hit the bar from close range with the last kick of the game.

"We made a couple of chances in the first half and a lot in the second. I thought it was only a matter of time until we scored." Chris Coleman

Event Line

30 ▪	Pennant (Ung Conduct)
31 ▪	**Legwinski (Foul)**
38 ▪	**Green (Foul)**
HALF TIME 0-0	
53 ▪	**Volz (Foul)**
67 ▪	Domi (Foul)
71 ⊙	**Davis S (Open Play)**
76 ⇄	Milner (Off) Johnson Si (On)
82 ▪	Caldwell (Foul)
83 ⊙	**Boa Morte (Indirect Free Kick)**
86 ⇄	**Hayles (Off) McBride (On)**
90 ▪	**Boa Morte (Ung Conduct)**
FULL TIME 2-0	

Statistics

Fulham				Leeds Utd
This Season	This Fixture		This Fixture	This Season
149	10	Shots On Target	3	92
157	10	Shots Off Target	4	133
8	0	Hit Woodwork	1	7
59	3	Caught Offside	4	89
119	4	Corners	7	139
413	17	Fouls	16	431
46%	53%	Possession	47%	44%

League Standings

Pos (pos before)	W	D	L	F	A	Pts
8 (9) Fulham	11	6	11	41	38	39
20 (20) Leeds	5	7	16	26	55	22

Premiership Milestone

75 Luis Boa Morte celebrated his 75th Premiership appearance for Fulham with a goal.

Sean Davis celebrates scoring

Chelsea 2
Fulham 1

Chelsea were made to work all the way in a keenly contested West London derby, which they won through Damien Duff's first-half strike.

The home side set the early pace, Frank Lampard exchanging a slick one-two with Hernan Crespo and racing into the area, only to pull his shot wide from a difficult angle in the fourth minute.

But Chelsea had to wait just three minutes more to take the lead, Eidur Gudjohnsen letting fly with a rising 25-yard shot which zipped past Edwin van der Sar and into the roof of the net.

Gudjohnsen threatened again on 11 minutes, this time volleying John Terry's lobbed header over the crossbar.

Lampard fouled Sean Davis just outside the area and Mark Pembridge stepped up to hit a powerful free kick from a central position which deflected off Jesper Gronkjaer before sailing home for a 19th minute equaliser. It was the first goal of the season for the Wales star.

Crespo played a fine ball in to set up Gudjohnsen, but Ian Pearce launched into a superbly timed tackle to save the day before blocking a dangerous Duff cross a minute later.

Match Details

Premiership
Saturday 20th March 2004
Venue: Stamford Bridge
Attendance: 41,169
Referee: N.S.Barry

Premiership Fixture History

Pl:**3** Draws:**1**	Wins	⚽	■	■
Chelsea	2	6	5	0
Fulham	**0**	**4**	**4**	**0**

Starting Line-up

Ambrosio
Gallas — Desailly — Terry (c) — Bridge
Gronkjaer — Geremi — Lampard — Duff
Gudjohnsen — Crespo

Hayles
Boa Morte — Malbranque
Pembridge — Legwinski (c) — S.Davis
Bocanegra — Pearce — Knight — Volz
van der Sar

Parker, J.Cole, Sullivan, Huth, Mutu.

John, McBride, Beasant, Goma, Djetou.

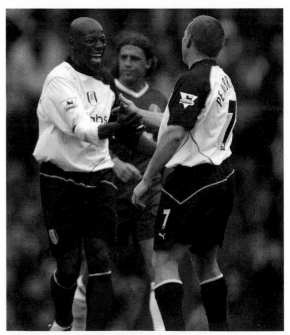

Mark Pembridge celebrates his goal with Luis Boa Morte

Geremi is pressured by Moritz Volz

7 ⊕ Gudjohnsen (Open Play)

19 ⊕ Pembridge (Direct Free Kick)

30 ⊕ Duff (Open Play)

HALF TIME 2-1

46 ⮂ Gronkjaer (Off) Parker (On)

48 ▌ Legwinski (Foul)

62 ⮂ Pembridge (Off) John (On)

66 ▌ Boa Morte (Foul)

70 ⮂ Duff (Off) Cole (On)

77 ⮂ Hayles (Off) McBride (On)

83 ▌ Parker (Foul)

FULL TIME 2-1

Statistics

Chelsea			Fulham	
This Season	This Fixture		This Fixture	This Season
156	8	Shots On Target	1	150
200	6	Shots Off Target	3	160
6	0	Hit Woodwork	0	8
90	3	Caught Offside	3	62
172	8	Corners	1	120
407	14	Fouls	16	429
53%	55%	Possession	45%	46%

League Standings

Pos (pos before)		W	D	L	F	A	Pts
2 (2)	Chelsea	20	4	5	52	22	64
9 (9)	Fulham	11	6	12	42	40	39

Premiership Milestone

Collins John made his Premiership debut, following his move from FC Twente.

Premiership Milestone

Mark Pembridge scored his first Premiership goal for Fulham.

Van der Sar got down well to block Duff's low angled drive on 30 minutes, but could only beat out Lampard's follow-up.

The loose ball cannoned off a defender and went straight to Duff, who comfortably placed it into an unguarded corner of the net.

Chelsea continued to press, as Geremi curled in a 38th minute free kick which van der Sar managed to turn away for a corner.

There was a surprise when the teams came out after the break, Claudio Ranieri having replaced the outstanding Gronkjaer with Scott Parker.

A great run and pass by Duff set up Lampard on 55 minutes, but he blazed way over from just inside the area.

We then had two good moves foiled in quick succession by narrow offside decisions.

Chelsea had a chance to clinch it on 67 minutes, but Geremi could do no more than roll a gentle effort into van der Sar's arms.

Our best chance of the second half arrived courtesy of substitute Collins John, who fired narrowly over from 30 yards 10 minutes from time.

"I thought Chelsea were there for the taking to be honest with you, and I'm disappointed we didn't do it. They will have to play better than that to have a good chance of beating Arsenal, but I'm sure they will step it up." Chris Coleman

Match Details

Premiership
Saturday 27th March 2004
Venue: City of Manchester Stadium
Attendance: 46,522
Referee: J.T.Winter

Premiership Fixture History

Pl:2 Draws:1 Wins ⚽ ▪ ▪

Manchester City	1	4	4	0
Fulham	**0**	**1**	**1**	**0**

Starting Line-up

Wanchope, Macken, Sinclair, Arason, Barton.

McBride, Beasant, Rehman, Inamoto, Sava.

Barry Hayles is chased by City's Michael Tarnat.

Manchester City 0
Fulham 0

We held on to deny City all three points in a tense encounter at the City of Manchester Stadium.

We were unable to threaten going forward and had to rely on the hands of Edwin van der Sar, who pushed a late snap-shot from Paulo Wanchope round the post before denying Jon Macken.

The first clear chance fell to City when Robbie Fowler met Antoine Sibierski's curling cross at the near post, but his flick didn't trouble van der Sar.

The Dutch keeper was called into action again soon after, this time keeping out Sibierski's header from a Michael Tarnat free kick, though a linesman's flag would have ruled it out in any case.

Sylvain Distin got within a whisker of meeting another dead-ball delivery from Tarnat, as he continued to be City's main attacking threat.

After a quiet first half, Shaun Wright-Phillips burst into life in the second, supplying a glorious cross to the far post which just evaded the diving Nicolas Anelka.

It was a minute short of the hour mark before David James

Carlos Bocanegra chases Shaun Wright-Phillips

Event Line

HALF TIME 0-0

60 ▮ Distin (Foul)

64 ⮂ Anelka (Off) Wanchope (On)

64 ⮂ Fowler (Off) Macken (On)

70 ⮂ **Hayles (Off) McBride (On)**

80 ⮂ Sibierski (Off) Sinclair (On)

FULL TIME 0-0

Statistics

Man City			Fulham	
This Season	This Fixture		This Fixture	This Season
169	3	Shots On Target	2	152
195	6	Shots Off Target	4	164
11	0	Hit Woodwork	0	8
100	7	Caught Offside	4	66
183	3	Corners	1	121
366	14	Fouls	12	441
49%	57%	Possession	43%	46%

was forced into his first meaningful save, a full-length parry from Sean Davis' angled effort which the impressive Richard Dunne was on hand to boot clear.

Stand-in City boss Arthur Cox decided to make wholesale changes up front in a bid to break the deadlock, replacing Fowler and Anelka with Macken and Wanchope.

The substitution almost paid immediate dividends, as Macken collected a long diagonal ball from Tarnat and ran at Alain Goma, who tangled with him in the area. Referee Jeff Winter ignored City's appeals for a penalty.

We looked to have won a penalty following Distin's reckless attempt to make up for gifting Luis Boa Morte possession by the touchline. But Winter again said no, much to the anger of Chris Coleman, who flew out of the dug-out to vent his frustration.

Wanchope's snap-shot brought the best out of van der Sar in the closing stages, and the keeper did well again to deny Macken from the resulting corner.

We almost nicked an unlikely winner in injury time when James spilled a Davis shot and had to scramble to recover with Steed Malbranque lurking.

League Standings

Pos (pos before)	W	D	L	F	A	Pts
15 (16) Man City	7	10	13	41	42	31
9 (9) Fulham	11	7	12	42	40	40

Premiership Milestone

75 Sean Davis made his 75th Premiership appearance.

"It wasn't pretty, and it may have looked a bit negative, but I'm not bothered about that, because we got the point we came for."
Chris Coleman

March Review

Month in Numbers

Games Played: **4**
Games Won: **1**
Games Drawn: **1**
Games Lost: **2**
Goals For: **4**
Goals Against: **4**

Results this Month

FA Cup, 06/03/2004
Man Utd 2-1 Fulham

Premiership, 13/03/2004
Fulham 2-0 Leeds

Premiership, 20/03/2004
Chelsea 2-1 Fulham

Premiership, 27/03/2004
Man City 0-0 Fulham

Premiership Table

Pos	(Feb)		Pl	W	D	L	F	A	Diff	Pts
1	(1)	Arsenal	30	22	8	0	58	20	+38	74
2	(2)	Chelsea	30	21	4	5	57	24	+33	67
3	(3)	Man Utd	30	19	5	6	56	30	+26	62
4	(6)	Liverpool	30	12	10	8	42	31	+11	46
5	(4)	Newcastle	30	11	12	7	41	31	+10	45
6	(9)	Birmingham	30	12	9	9	37	36	+1	45
7	(7)	Aston Villa	30	12	7	11	38	35	+3	43
8	(5)	Charlton	30	12	7	11	41	39	+2	43
9	**(8)**	**Fulham**	**30**	**11**	**7**	**12**	**42**	**40**	**+2**	**40**
10	(12)	Southampton	30	10	9	11	30	28	+2	39
11	(13)	Middlesbro	30	10	8	12	35	39	-4	38
12	(10)	Tottenham	30	11	4	15	40	47	-7	37
13	(11)	Bolton	30	9	10	11	34	46	-12	37
14	(14)	Everton	30	8	10	12	36	41	-5	34
15	(16)	Man City	30	7	10	13	41	42	-1	31
16	(15)	Blackburn	30	8	7	15	42	48	-6	31
17	(17)	Portsmouth	30	8	6	16	32	45	-13	30
18	(19)	Leicester	30	5	13	12	39	52	-13	28
19	(20)	Leeds	30	6	7	17	29	60	-31	25
20	(18)	Wolves	30	5	9	16	26	62	-36	24

Premiership Progression

Win: ■ Draw: ■ Loss: ■ League position: **8** League position 2002-03: **8** Home fixtures in black

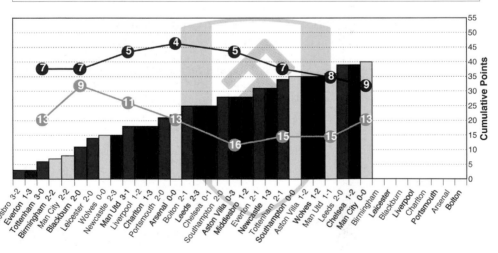

March Review

Premiership Performance

	March	03-04
Shots On Target	13	152
Shots Off Target	17	164
Hit Woodwork	0	8
Clean Sheets	2	10
Failed To Score	1	6
Caught Offside	10	66
Corners	6	121
Own Goals For	0	0
Own Goals Against	0	1

Goals Resulting From

	March		03-04	
	F	A	F	A
Open Play	1	2	32	25
Set Piece	2	0	10	14

How Goals Scored

	March		03-04	
	F	A	F	A
Right Foot	1	0	19	18
Left Foot	1	2	21	15
Header	1	0	2	6

When Goals Scored

	March		03-04	
	F	A	F	A
First Half	1	2	16	21
Second Half	2	0	26	18

Top Goal Scorers

	March	03-04
L. Saha	0	13
L. Boa Morte	1	8
S. Malbranque	0	5
B. Hayles	0	4
S. Davis	1	4

Top Goal Assists

	March	03-04
S. Malbranque	1	12
L. Saha	0	5
L. Boa Morte	0	4
L. Clark	0	4
B. Hayles	0	3
S. Davis	1	3

Player of the Month

Zat Knight

Goals: **0** Assists: **1**

Two clean sheets in three games owed much to the form of the ever-improving Zat Knight. The big defender helped keep Alan Smith and Mark Viduka at bay against Leeds, and even had time to get forward and set up an 83rd-minute goal. It took two special strikes to sink Fulham at Chelsea, but the defence, and Knight in particular, were soon back on song, blunting a dangerous Manchester City attack in a 0-0 draw. The Solihull-born defender also demonstrated his confidence on the ball, striking the crossbar from 35-yards in a cup tie at Old Trafford.

Fulham 0
Birmingham City 0

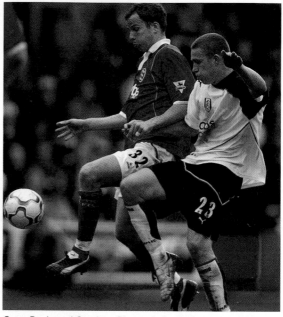

Sean Davis and Stephen Clemence battle for possession.

Match Details

Premiership
Saturday 3rd April 2004
Venue: Loftus Road
Attendance: 14,667
Referee: M.A.Riley

Premiership Fixture History

	Pl:2 Draws:1	Wins ⚫	⬛	⬛
Fulham	0	0	7	0
Birmingham City	1	1	8	1

Starting Line-up

van der Sar

Volz   Knight   Goma   Bocanegra

S.Davis   Djetou   Legwinski (c)

Malbranque   Boa Morte
          Hayles

Morrison   Forssell

Lazaridis   Hughes   Savage   Johnson

Grainger   Upson   Cunningham (c)   Martin Taylor

Maik Taylor

McBride, Pearce, Crossley, Inamoto, Petta.

Clemence, John, Clapham, Bennett, Tebily.

It took a sublime performance from Birmingham keeper Maik Taylor to earn his side a point at Loftus Road.

He made three brilliant first-half saves to deny Barry Hayles, Steed Malbranque and Luis Boa Morte.

Referee Mike Riley was the busiest man in West London, dishing out six bookings to take the tally from our last four league matches with Birmingham to 23 yellows and five reds.

Martin Djetou had the game's first shot, but his right-foot effort ballooned into the upper tier 20 yards wide of the target.

Robbie Savage went much closer at the other end with four minutes on the clock, robbing Moritz Volz before smashing a ferocious 22-yard drive against the crossbar.

Only heroics from Taylor prevented us going in front on 18 minutes.

Hayles rose to meet Sean Davis' free kick and power a header which Taylor managed to parry. Sylvain Legwinski chipped the ball back across goal, only for Djetou to head wide.

Clinton Morrison had two sights of goal as half-time approached, but he blazed his first shot high and wide before

Martin Djetou is challenged by Birmingham's Robbie Savage

completely missing the ball with his second chance.

We showed greater accuracy in attack seven minutes before the break, but were thwarted by some strong Birmingham defending.

Taylor parried Malbranque's fierce drive before leaping to his feet to save Boa Morte's effort on the rebound. Matthew Upson then blocked Malbranque's follow-up shot.

There was plenty of niggle in this contest and a flashpoint came four minutes after the break.

Malbranque flicked a boot at Savage after he'd bundled him over and the Welshman responded by seizing Malbranque by the scruff of the neck. Both were booked for their actions.

Birmingham were still struggling to create anything in front of goal, with a blocked effort from Mikael Forssell the closest they came.

Referee Riley turned down a penalty appeal when Boa Morte stumbled following Stan Lazaridis' challenge.

Chris Coleman introduced centre-back Ian Pearce as a makeshift striker late on, but his only contribution was a weak shot which trickled into Taylor's grasp.

Birmingham midfielder Bryan Hughes found space to shoot from 20 yards, but his effort fizzed wide.

"I changed things at half-time, and maybe that was my fault. I placed too much emphasis on getting the ball forward, without the extra pass we usually use." Chris Coleman

Statistics

Fulham			Birmingham	
This Season	This Fixture		This Fixture	This Season
156	4	Shots On Target	0	135
167	3	Shots Off Target	4	162
8	0	Hit Woodwork	1	9
67	1	Caught Offside	4	65
124	3	Corners	2	170
468	27	Fouls	19	446
46%	52%	Possession	48%	46%

League Standings

Pos (pos before)	W	D	L	F	A	Pts
10 (9) Fulham	11	8	12	42	40	41
6 (6) Birmingham	12	10	9	37	36	46

Premiership
Saturday 10th April 2004
Venue: Walkers Stadium
Attendance: 28,392
Referee: P.Walton

Premiership Fixture History

	Pl:**2** Draws:**1**	Wins ⚽	◼	◼
Leicester City	0	0	4	0
Fulham	1	2	3	0

Starting Line-up

Walker
Scimeca   Dabizas   Heath   Thatcher
Scowcroft   Freund   Izzet (c)   Guppy
Bent   Dickov

Hayles
Boa Morte   Malbranque
Legwinski (c)   Djetou   S.Davis
Bocanegra   Goma   Knight   Volz
van der Sar

Nalis, Canero,   John, McBride,
Stewart, McKinlay,   Crossley, Pearce,
Benjamin.   Petta.

Moritz Volz gets up against Muzzy Izzet

Leicester City 0
Fulham 2

Two goals from Collins John powered us to our first league win on the road since the 3-1 triumph at Old Trafford on October 25.

We were the first to threaten, as Sean Davis knocked in a right-wing free kick to the far post. Zat Knight headed goalwards, but Foxes keeper Ian Walker made the save.

Steed Malbranque was the next to chance his luck with a fierce 20-yard drive which fizzed narrowly high and wide.

Sylvain Legwinski went close in the 23rd minute, but his close-range effort was courageously blocked by Steffen Freund. The Foxes midfielder's late challenge on Moritz Volz then earned him a yellow card.

Malbranque blazed over the crossbar from 18 yards before Luis Boa Morte was cautioned for a late, lunging challenge on Walker.

Leicester might have done better five minutes before the interval, as Marcus Bent collected on the right and sent the ball into the penalty area, only for James Scowcroft to spoon well over.

Paul Dickov was unlucky in the 52nd minute when his shot

Collins John celebrates after scoring one of his two goals

25 ■ Freund (Foul)

38 ■ Boa Morte (Foul)

45 ■ Dickov (Foul)

HALF TIME 0-0

62 ⇄ Hayles (Off) John (On)

66 ⊙ John (Open Play)

71 ⇄ Malbranque (Off) McBride (On)

74 ⇄ Freund (Off) Nalis (On)

80 ⇄ Dabizas (Off) Canero (On)

89 ⊙ John (Open Play)

FULL TIME 0-2

Statistics

Leicester City				Fulham	
This Season	This Fixture			This Fixture	This Season
152	3	Shots On Target	3		159
160	6	Shots Off Target	5		172
11	1	Hit Woodwork	0		8
103	3	Caught Offside	8		75
178	15	Corners	4		128
494	15	Fouls	**20**		488
45%	48%	Possession	**52%**		46%

League Standings

Pos (pos before)	W	D	L	F	A	Pts
19 (18) Leicester	5	13	14	41	57	28
8 (10) Fulham	12	8	12	44	40	44

Premiership Milestone

Collins John scored his first Premiership goals.

battered the underside of the bar.

Muzzy Izzet thought he'd broken the deadlock when he put the ball in the back of the net after stealing it from Edwin van der Sar.

The Leicester skipper seized the ball when the Dutch keeper dropped it, but the referee blew for an infringement.

There was more frustration for the hosts moments later, as Dickov raced clear and unleashed a low drive which was spectacularly saved by van der Sar with a dive to his left.

We grabbed the opener on 66 minutes, Malbranque chipping forward for the sprinting John, who beat Walker to the bouncing ball and lifted it into a gaping net. It was his first goal in a Fulham shirt.

A last-ditch intervention by Nikos Dabizas prevented us going further ahead after Volz had worked his way into the box and produced a powerful close-range shot.

Leicester poured forward late in the game and were caught on the break in the 89th minute when Boa Morte raced down the left channel and slid the ball through Ben Thatcher's legs for John to coolly slot home.

"Prior to our first goal we were under pressure, so I was really pleased with the way Collins went about his business."
Chris Coleman

Fulham 3
Blackburn Rovers 4

Match Details

Premiership
Monday 12th April 2004
Venue: Loftus Road
Attendance: 13,981
Referee: M.L.Dean

Premiership Fixture History

Pl:3 Draws:0	Wins	⊙	■	■
Fulham	1	5	3	0
Blackburn Rovers	2	8	5	1

Starting Line-up

van der Sar
Volz   Knight   Goma   Bocanegra
S.Davis   Djetou   Legwinski (c)
Malbranque   Boa Morte
John
Stead   Cole
Douglas   Tugay (c)   Andresen   Flitcroft
Gresko   Short   Amoruso   Neill
Friedel

Petta, McBride,   Emerton,Gallagher,
Hayles, Crossley,   Enckelman, Reid,
Pearce.   Johansson.

Sylvain Legwinski and Blackburn's Gary Flitcroft.

Blackburn halted their freefall towards relegation with a rollercoaster victory at Loftus Road.

Rovers, who had just suffered three straight defeats, twice lost the lead before Jonathan Stead's 75th minute strike put them ahead for good.

The visitors opened the scoring on 23 minutes.

Kerimoglu Tugay's magnificent 40-yard curling pass released Andy Cole, who controlled with his chest before smashing a ferocious close-range volley past Edwin van der Sar.

But we were level just three minutes later, as Collins John – making his full debut – beat Carlos Bocanegra to the ball following Sean Davis' free kick and bundled it over the line.

Brad Friedel saved two Zat Knight headers from set-pieces to keep it even as the interval approached.

But the American was beaten on the stroke of half-time, as John nipped in ahead of Vratislav Gresko to touch home a Davis free kick from the right for a 2-1 lead.

Rovers roared back into the lead after the break with two

Carlos Bocanegra beats Garry Flitcroft to the ball

Event Line

23 ⊙ Cole (Open Play)

26 ⊙ John (Indirect Free Kick)

45 ⊙ John (Indirect Free Kick)

HALF TIME 2-1

49 ⊙ Douglas (Open Play)

51 ⊙ Amoruso (Indirect Free Kick)

60 ⊙ Boa Morte (Open Play)

75 ⊙ Stead (Open Play)

79 ⇄ Davis S (Off) Petta (On)

84 ⇄ Malbranque (Off) McBride (On)

87 ⇄ John (Off) Hayles (On)

89 ⇄ Cole (Off) Emerton (On)

90 ⇄ Stead (Off) Gallagher (On)

FULL TIME 3-4

goals in as many minutes.

On 49 minutes, Garry Flitcroft flicked on a throw for Jonathan Douglas to volley into the top corner from eight yards. It was the Irish midfielder's first goal for the club on his 17th appearance.

Two minutes later, Lorenzo Amoruso smacked a 30-yard free kick which van der Sar could only palm into the net.

It was exciting, end-to-end stuff, and we pulled back to 3-3 on the hour with a stunning goal.

Martin Djetou broke up a Rovers attack and the ball fell to Luis Boa Morte, 25 yards inside his own half. The Portuguese winger sprinted upfield, exchanging passes with John before capping a superb move with a cool finish from just inside the box.

But this topsy-turvy match took another twist in the 75th minute when Rovers took the lead for the third and final time.

Stead played a one-two with Cole and let fly from 20 yards, his powerful shot squirming under van der Sar's body and into the net.

With time running out, John skied a right-foot shot well over the bar and Moritz Volz hit a 20-yard screamer that Friedel did well to gather.

"To score three goals against a team fighting relegation, but concede four, is something I can't explain." Chris Coleman

Statistics

	Fulham			Blackburn	
	This Season	This Fixture		This Fixture	This Season
166		**7**	Shots On Target	9	158
178		**6**	Shots Off Target	4	205
8		**0**	Hit Woodwork	0	7
77		**2**	Caught Offside	5	130
134		**6**	Corners	1	203
502		**14**	Fouls	17	474
46%		**51%**	Possession	49%	48%

League Standings

Pos (pos before)	W	D	L	F	A	Pts
10 (8) Fulham	12	8	13	47	44	44
16 (16) Blackburn	9	7	17	47	57	34

Premiership Milestone

75 Barry Hayles made his 75th appearance in the Premiership.

Match Details

Premiership
Saturday 17th April 2004
Venue: Anfield
Attendance: 42,042
Referee: S.G.Bennett

Premiership Fixture History

Pl:3	Draws:2	Wins ☺	■	■
Liverpool	1	2	1	0
Fulham	**0**	**0**	**5**	**0**

Starting Line-up

Baros, Diouf,
Heskey, Murphy,
Luzi Bernardi.

McBride, Inamoto,
Rehman, Crossley,
Hayles.

Moritz Volz and Bruno Cheyrou

Liverpool 0
Fulham 0

Liverpool's chances of making it into European competition next season took another crushing blow as we held them to a goalless draw at Anfield.

Vladimir Smicer had the best early chance, but his shot from the edge of the box was a tame effort that was dealt with easily by Edwin van der Sar.

The Liverpool midfielder had another chance a minute later when the ball bounced over Michael Owen and came to him at the far post, but his shot deflected over for a corner.

Owen then flashed a shot just wide from the edge of the box before we went desperately close, Moritz Volz's strike deflecting narrowly over off Sami Hyypia.

Luis Boa Morte had a swerving shot just tipped over by Jerzy Dudek before Collins John struck the keeper with a poor effort when unmarked six yards out, the rebound hacked off the line by John Arne Riise.

Liverpool were handed the perfect chance to break the deadlock five minutes into the second half when referee Steve Bennett gave a penalty for handball against Bobby Petta.

Skipper Steven Gerrard took over penalty duty from Owen, who had been struggling from the spot, but his blast was well saved by van der Sar.

Harry Kewell had a great chance from five yards out, but his effort was well blocked. The Australian then fired in a stinging shot that van der Sar did well to beat away at his near post.

A counter-attack opened space for Steed Malbranque, but his overhead kick was blocked by Jamie Carragher.

The Reds piled forward in search of an opener, substitute Milan Baros setting up Owen, who fired what looked a certain goal before Volz's superb intervention.

Emile Heskey came off the bench as Gerard Houllier launched a desperate bid for the win, and the former Leicester man went within an inch of doing the trick, just missing after Gerrard's cross.

Baros had a goalbound effort blocked by a desperate lunge as we dug deep to hang on for a point.

"If we finish in the top eight it's a triumph, but we can still make Europe ourselves. It is very exciting for us and there is still plenty to play for. If we beat Charlton next week anything can happen." Chris Coleman

Event Line

HALF TIME 0-0

49 ▮ **Bocanegra (Foul)**

51 ▮ **John (Dissent)**

60 ⇄ Cheyrou (Off) Baros (On)

72 ▮ **Goma (Foul)**

74 ⇄ **John (Off) McBride (On)**

76 ⇄ Kewell (Off) Heskey (On)

76 ⇄ Smicer (Off) Diouf (On)

77 ⇄ **Bocanegra (Off) Inamoto (On)**

89 ⇄ **Petta (Off) Rehman (On)**

FULL TIME 0-0

Statistics

Liverpool			Fulham	
This Season	This Fixture		This Fixture	This Season
214	3	Shots On Target	2	168
258	11	Shots Off Target	6	184
12	0	Hit Woodwork	0	8
105	2	Caught Offside	4	81
239	13	Corners	7	141
399	17	Fouls	13	515
52%	61%	Possession	39%	46%

League Standings

Pos (pos before)		W	D	L	F	A	Pts
4 (4)	Liverpool	13	11	10	48	36	50
10 (10)	Fulham	12	9	13	47	44	45

Premiership Milestone

Last-minute substitute Zesh Rehman made his Premiership debut.

Carlos Bocanegra and Harry Kewell play it their way

Fulham 2
Charlton Athletic 0

Premiership
Saturday 24th April 2004
Venue: Loftus Road
Attendance: 16,585
Referee: M.D.Messias

Premiership Fixture History

Pl:3 Draws:1	Wins	⊙	■	■
Fulham	2	3	4	0
Charlton Athletic	0	0	4	0

Starting Line-up

van der Sar

Volz   Pearce   Goma   Bocanegra

Malbranque   Legwinski (c)   Djetou   Petta

Boa Morte   John

Cole   Euell

Konchesky   Jensen   Holland (c)   Stuart

Powell   Hreidarsson   Fortune   Young

Kiely

S.Davis, McBride, Inamoto, Crossley, Knight.

Perry, Johansson, Di Canio, Royce, Kishishev.

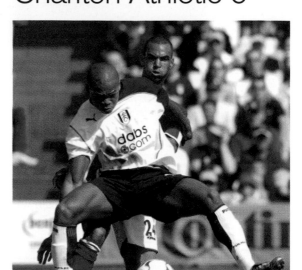

Collins John moves ahead of Jonathan Fortune

Sean Davis slammed home a sensational volley to get us back in the race for Europe.

The midfielder, dropped for the previous weekend's 0-0 draw at Liverpool as punishment for breaking a late-night curfew over Easter, fired home from 20 yards in the 64th minute.

We finished the game on 48 points, within touching distance of the Champions League and UEFA Cup.

The match got off to a frantic start, with chances aplenty at both ends in the opening quarter-hour.

Charlton were lucky to escape a penalty call after just 10 seconds when Collins John tumbled in the box after Steed Malbranque's pass.

Thirty seconds later the ball was up the other end, as Edwin van der Sar made a smart save to deny Claus Jensen.

We hit back with a Luis Boa Morte shot which flashed high and wide before Jonathan Fortune robbed John just as he was about to pull the trigger in front of goal.

Graham Stuart and Jensen then both fired narrowly wide

Sean Davis celebrates scoring Fulham's second

Event Line

18 ⊙ **Malbranque (Penalty)**

HALF TIME 1-0

46 ⇄ **Petta (Off) Davis S (On)**

49 ▢ Powell (Foul)

54 ▢ **Volz (Foul)**

64 ⊙ **Davis S (Open Play)**

69 ⇄ **John (Off) McBride (On)**

72 ⇄ Cole (Off) Johansson (On)

72 ⇄ Powell (Off) Perry (On)

72 ⇄ Stuart (Off) Di Canio (On)

76 ⇄ **Boa Morte (Off) Inamoto (On)**

FULL TIME 2-0

before we made the breakthrough on 18 minutes.

Boa Morte raced past Hermann Hreidarsson onto a through-ball and was sent sprawling by Dean Kiely.

Referee Matt Messias pointed to the spot and Malbranque punished Kiely, sending him the wrong way to put us in front.

Charlton had a great shout for a spot-kick of their own turned down six minutes later, as Messias ruled that Martin Djetou had accidentally handled when Luke Young hooked the ball against his arm.

Malbranque almost scored a brilliant second just after the half-hour, jinking into space for a shot which Kiely parried.

Messias enraged the away supporters by waving away another Charlton penalty shout after Alain Goma swung a leg across Jason Euell's chest.

We were quick out of the blocks after the break, Sylvain Legwinski smashing a 20-yarder just over the top.

We doubled our lead in the 64th minute in spectacular fashion.

Boa Morte shrugged off Matt Holland on the halfway line and raced towards goal before rolling the ball across to Davis, 25 yards out.

Davis miscontrolled and accidentally flicked the ball into the air, but made amends as he connected with a dipping volley which arched into the bottom corner.

"We needed that result if we were to keep our hopes alive of finishing in the top six."
Chris Coleman

Statistics

Fulham			Charlton	
This Season	This Fixture		This Fixture	This Season
172	4	Shots On Target	2	152
189	5	Shots Off Target	6	192
8	0	Hit Woodwork	0	15
84	3	Caught Offside	4	116
145	4	Corners	7	188
531	16	Fouls	14	479
46%	56%	Possession	44%	46%

League Standings

Pos (pos before)	W	D	L	F	A	Pts
7 (10) Fulham	13	9	13	49	44	48
8 (7) Charlton	13	9	13	44	45	48

Premiership Milestone

125 Steed Malbranque's goal was Fulham's 125th in the Premiership.

April Review

Month in Numbers

Games Played: **5**
Games Won: **2**
Games Drawn: **2**
Games Lost: **1**
Goals For: **7**
Goals Against: **4**

Results this Month

Premiership, 03/04/2004
Fulham 0-0 Birmingham
Premiership, 10/04/2004
Leicester 0-2 Fulham
Premiership, 12/04/2004
Fulham 3-4 Blackburn
Premiership, 17/04/2004
Liverpool 0-0 Fulham
Premiership, 24/04/2004
Fulham 2-0 Charlton

Premiership Table

Pos	(Mar)		Pl	W	D	L	F	A	Diff	Pts
1	(1)	Arsenal	34	24	10	0	69	24	+45	82
2	(2)	Chelsea	35	22	6	7	61	29	+32	72
3	(3)	Man Utd	35	22	5	8	61	33	+28	71
4	(4)	Liverpool	35	14	11	10	49	36	+13	53
5	(5)	Newcastle	34	13	14	7	47	34	+13	53
6	(7)	Aston Villa	35	14	10	11	46	41	+5	52
7	**(9)**	**Fulham**	**35**	**13**	**9**	**13**	**49**	**44**	**+5**	**48**
8	(8)	Charlton	35	13	9	13	44	45	-1	48
9	(6)	Birmingham	35	12	12	11	42	44	-2	48
10	(13)	Bolton	35	12	11	12	42	52	-10	47
11	(10)	Southampton	34	12	9	13	39	35	+4	45
12	(11)	Middlesbro'	35	12	9	14	41	44	-3	45
13	(16)	Blackburn	35	11	7	17	49	57	-8	40
14	(17)	Portsmouth	34	11	7	16	39	48	-9	40
15	(14)	Everton	35	9	12	14	42	48	-6	39
16	(12)	Tottenham	35	11	6	18	44	56	-12	39
17	(15)	Man City	35	7	14	14	48	51	-3	35
18	(19)	Leeds	35	8	8	19	36	71	-35	32
19	(18)	Leicester	35	5	14	16	42	60	-18	29
20	(20)	Wolves	35	6	11	18	35	73	-38	29

Premiership Progression

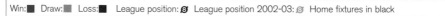

Win:■ Draw:■ Loss:■ League position: **8** League position 2002-03: **9** Home fixtures in black

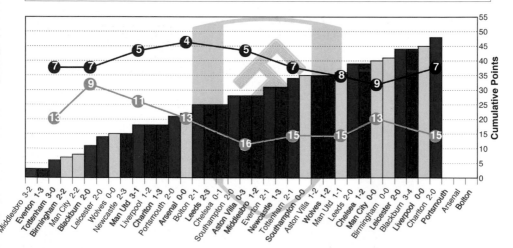

April Review

Premiership Performance

	April	03-04
Shots On Target	20	172
Shots Off Target	25	189
Hit Woodwork	0	8
Clean Sheets	4	14
Failed To Score	2	8
Caught Offside	18	84
Corners	24	145
Own Goals For	0	0
Own Goals Against	0	1

Goals Resulting From

	April		03-04	
	F	A	F	A
Open Play	4	3	36	28
Set Piece	3	1	13	15

How Goals Scored

	April		03-04	
	F	A	F	A
Right Foot	5	4	24	22
Left Foot	1	0	22	15
Header	1	0	3	6

When Goals Scored

	April		03-04	
	F	A	F	A
First Half	3	1	19	22
Second Half	4	3	30	21

Top Goal Scorers

	April	03-04
L. Saha	0	13
L. Boa Morte	1	9
S. Malbranque	1	6
S. Davis	1	5
C. John	4	4
B. Hayles	0	4

Top Goal Assists

	April	03-04
S. Malbranque	3	15
L. Boa Morte	3	7
L. Saha	0	5
L. Clark	0	4
B. Hayles	0	3
S. Davis	0	3

Player of the Month

Collins John

Goals: **4** Assists: **1**

While the defence layed the foundations for a solid month, with four clean sheets in five games, it was the Liberian striker who stole the headlines. John came off the bench to net both goals in the 2-0 win at Leicester, a performance which was rewarded with his first start, against Blackburn two days later. Chris Coleman's faith was rewarded with two more goals, as well as an assist. John brought a real physical presence to the attack, and seemed to produce his best form when playing as a lone striker.

Portsmouth 1
Fulham1

A late equaliser by substitute Brian McBride earned us a draw at Fratton Park.

Portsmouth were pleased with the result, the point guaranteeing their Premiership status for next season.

The home side made the early running, a fine through-ball by Matt Taylor almost putting Aiyegbeni Yakubu in after just two minutes.

Two minutes later, Nigel Quashie's goalbound shot was blocked by Alain Goma following a short corner.

Goma was well placed again soon afterwards, clearing up when Edwin van der Sar spilt Quashie's overhit pass into the area.

On 11 minutes, Luis Boa Morte managed a shot on target from 18 yards after linking with Martin Djetou, but it was an easy take for Shaka Hislop.

Portsmouth wasted an excellent chance on 17 minutes when the dangerous Lomana Tresor Lua Lua escaped down the right and fired over a great cross which Yakubu headed over the bar.

With 22 minutes gone, the home side were suddenly caught short on their left flank, where Sean Davis would have moved in

Match Details

Premiership
Saturday 1st May 2004
Venue: Fratton Park
Attendance: 20,065
Referee: S.W.Dunn

Premiership Fixture History

	Pl:**1** Draws:**1**	Wins	⚽	■	■
Portsmouth	0	1	1	0
Fulham	**0**	**1**	**4**	**0**

Starting Line-up

Hislop

Primus   De Zeeuw (c)   Stefanovic   Taylor

Stone   Faye   Smertin   Quashie

Lua Lua   Yabuku

Boa Morte

Malbranque   Inamoto

Legwinski (c)   Djetou   S.Davis

Bocanegra   Goma   Pearce   Volz

van der Sar

Duffy, Sheringham, Wapenaar, Harper, Berkovic.
McBride, John, Crossley, Hudson, Petta.

Moritz Volz gets ahead of Matthew Taylor

Yakubu Aiyegbeni of Portsmouth gets ahead of Alain Goma

Event Line

22 ⚽ Primus (Off) Duffy (On)

40 ▉ Legwinski (Foul)

42 ▉ Bocanegra (Foul)

HALF TIME 0-0

52 ▉ Faye (Foul)

57 ▉ Inamoto (Ung Conduct)

77 ⚽ Djetou (Off) McBride (On)

80 ⊙ Yakubu (Corner)

84 ▉ Goma (Foul)

85 ⚽ Boa Morte (Off) John (On)

85 ⊙ McBride (Open Play)

90 ⚽ Yabuku (Off) Sheringham (On)

FULL TIME 1-1

unopposed on a Boa Morte pass but for Dejan Stefanovic's brilliant recovery tackle.

A long ball forward wasn't exactly Pompey's style, but it found Lua Lua in good space in the area and he should have done better than screw his shot across the face of goal on 34 minutes.

He almost made amends two minutes later, his shot from an almost impossible angle on the right cannoning off the near post.

We began the second half in sparkling style, Davis striking the underside of the bar from 18 yards after less than 30 seconds.

Alexei Smertin hit a powerful drive, only to see van der Sar collect comfortably at head height.

Sylvain Legwinski then scooped a good chance over after muscling his way through.

Steed Malbranque's 71st-minute free kick was deflected over and the resulting corner saw Junichi Inamoto drive just wide.

Portsmouth stuck to their task and 10 minutes from time Yakubu jumped on a slip by van der Sar to knock the ball in.

Five minutes later, McBride stunned the hosts with a savage drive from 20 yards to level matters.

The American had a chance to clinch it in stoppage time, but miscued in front of a gaping net.

Statistics

Portsmouth			Fulham
This Season	This Fixture		This Fixture	This Season
150	5	Shots On Target	3	175
190	10	Shots Off Target	6	195
9	1	Hit Woodwork	1	9
136	6	Caught Offside	1	85
177	10	Corners	3	148
550	15	Fouls	16	547
46%	45%	Possession	55%	46%

League Standings

Pos (pos before)		W	D	L	F	A	Pts
14 (14)	Portsmouth	11	8	16	40	49	41
7 (7)	Fulham	13	10	13	50	45	49

**"Whilst Boa isn't really a target man, Brian McBride is and we were able to build attacks off him a little bit better. Although we left it late, Brian came on and scored so it paid off."
Chris Coleman**

Match Details

Premiership
Sunday 9th May 2004
Venue: Loftus Road
Attendance: 18,102
Referee: M.L.Dean

Premiership Fixture History

Pl:3 Draws:0	Wins ☉	■	■
Fulham	0	1	5	0
Arsenal	3	5	9	0

Sylvain Legwinski gets to grips with Thierry Henry

Starting Line-up

van der Sar
Volz Pearce Goma Bocanegra
Inamoto Djetou Legwinski
S.Davis Malbranque
Boa Morte

Henry Reyes
Pires Parlour Vieira (c) Ljungberg
Cole Campbell Toure Lauren
Lehmann

John, McBride, Crossley, Hudson, Petta.

Aliadiere, Clichy, Keown, Stack, Bergkamp.

Fulham 0
Arsenal 1

A goal from Jose Antonio Reyes extended Arsenal's incredible unbeaten league run since the start of the season to 37 games.

The Gunners behaved like imposing gatecrashers for the first 10 minutes, as they controlled the game.

Edwin van der Sar was quickly forced into a smart save at the feet of Freddie Ljungberg, who had raced onto Ray Parlour's through-ball. But the Dutchman was to be horribly embarrassed shortly afterwards.

Martin Djetou's backpass should have been easily dealt with, but van der Sar miscontrolled the ball.

The keeper then tried to sidestep Reyes, but was tackled and could only watch as the Spaniard slotted the ball into the goal.

We regrouped and started to dominate possession, with Steed Malbranque and Sean Davis leading by example in midfield.

Luis Boa Morte managed to burst clear onto Junichi Inamoto's through-ball, only for Jens Lehmann to make an excellent reaction block.

Malbranque was a presence on the left, curling one effort just wide, having another saved by Lehmann and then flashing an overhead kick over the bar.

Chris Coleman clearly felt he needed more attacking options, however, as he introduced Brian McBride and Collins John for Inamoto and Djetou with 32 minutes left.

Arsenal continued to hold firm at the back and were always dangerous on the break, with the lively Reyes striking the side netting from the edge of the penalty area.

Jeremie Aliadiere, making his 10th league appearance of the season to guarantee a Premiership winner's medal, replaced the Spaniard with 19 minutes left.

Arsenal were not at their most fluent, but their determination to remain unbeaten was clear, as Ashley Cole flung himself to block a drive by Sylvain Legwinski.

After Moritz Volz fired a stinging drive just past the far post, Gael Clichy was quickly brought on in place of Robert Pires to add more defensive strength to Arsenal's left flank.

Malbranque then wasted two good chances, blasting a free kick from the edge of the box against the wall before just failing to connect at the far post from four yards out.

After finishing the season unbeaten away from home, just a home game against relegated Leicester City next week stood between the Gunners and an unbeaten Premiership season.

"I thought we deserved at least a draw. They weren't under par – we gifted them a goal."
Chris Coleman

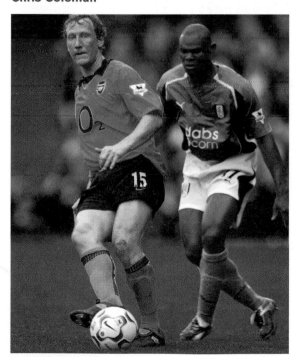

Martin Djetou and Ray Parlour

Season Review 2003-04

Event Line

9 ⊙ Reyes (Open Play)

HALF TIME 0-1

52 ▮ Vieira (Foul)

58 ⇄ **Djetou (Off) John (On)**

58 ⇄ **Inamoto (Off) McBride (On)**

69 ▮ Henry (Foul)

71 ⇄ Reyes (Off) Aliadiere (On)

78 ⇄ Pires (Off) Clichy (On)

84 ▮ Parlour (Dissent)

87 ⇄ Ljungberg (Off) Keown (On)

89 ▮ **Davis S (Dissent)**

FULL TIME 0-1

Statistics

Fulham			Arsenal	
This Season	This Fixture		This Fixture	This Season
177	2	Shots On Target	5	223
206	11	Shots Off Target	3	206
9	0	Hit Woodwork	0	17
86	1	Caught Offside	3	110
154	6	Corners	7	195
560	13	Fouls	20	525
47%	50%	Possession	50%	54%

League Standings

Pos (pos before)	W	D	L	F	A	Pts
9 (9) Fulham	13	10	14	50	46	49
1 (1) Arsenal	25	12	0	71	25	87

Premiership Milestone

50 Martin Djetou made his 50th appearance in the Premiership.

Fulham Football Club Official Yearbook 2004-05   113

Bolton Wanderers 0
Fulham 2

Brian McBride grabbed a brace to spoil Bolton's end-of-season party at the Reebok Stadium.

The American striker scored in either half to end the home team's five-match unbeaten run.

The victory rounded off a splendid campaign for manager Chris Coleman in his first season in charge, as he steered us to our highest ever finishing position in the top-flight.

Bolton also enjoyed their best top-flight finish.

We had a scare in the first minute when Jay-Jay Okocha launched a long throw into the area. The ball was only half cleared and Nicky Hunt whipped in a shot that went narrowly wide.

Carlos Bocanegra tried to release Sean Davis, but Wanderers keeper Jussi Jaaskelainen raced out to intercept.

A delightful move between Hunt and Kevin Nolan ended with Bocanegra making a hasty clearance.

Per Frandsen was then marginally off target with a shot from the edge of the area.

Kevin Davies should have put Bolton ahead in the 17th minute.

Okocha launched the ball forward and Alain Goma slipped,

Match Details

Premiership
Saturday 15th May 2004
Venue: Reebok Stadium
Attendance: 27,383
Referee: G.P.Barber

Premiership Fixture History

	Pl	Draws	Wins		
Pl:**3** Draws:**2** Wins					
Bolton Wanderers	0	0	3	0	
Fulham	1	2	4	0	

Starting Line-up

Jaaskelainen
Hunt   Thome   N'Gotty   Charlton
Frandsen   Campo   Okocha (c)
Nolan   Djorkaeff
Davies

McBride
Boa Morte   Malbranque
Legwinski (c)   Djetou   S.Davis
Bocanegra   Goma   Pearce   Volz
van der Sar

Gardner, Pedersen, Stelios, Ricketts, Barness.

John, Crossley, Hudson, Inamoto, Petta.

Sylvain Legwinski joins in Brian McBride's goal celebrations

Luis Boa Morte is chased by Nicky Hunt

Event Line

45 ⚽ **McBride (Open Play)**

HALF TIME 0-1

46 🔄 Charlton (Off) Gardner (On)

59 🔄 Djorkaeff (Off) Pedersen (On)

60 ▮ Davies (Foul)

71 🔄 Frandsen (Off) Stelios (On)

78 ⚽ **McBride (Open Play)**

86 ▮ **Boa Morte (Ung Conduct)**

90 🔄 McBride (Off) John (On)

FULL TIME 0-2

Statistics

	Bolton			Fulham	
	This Season	This Fixture		This Fixture	This Season
	199	5	Shots On Target	4	181
	286	12	Shots Off Target	2	208
	14	1	Hit Woodwork	0	9
	103	4	Caught Offside	2	88
	232	10	Corners	3	157
	513	12	Fouls	18	578
	45%	54%	Possession	46%	47%

League Standings

Pos (pos before)		W	D	L	F	A	Pts
8 (7)	Bolton	14	11	13	48	56	53
9 (9)	Fulham	14	10	14	52	46	52

Premiership Milestone

100 Fulham skipper Sylvain Legwinski made his 100th Premiership appearance.

leaving Davies with a clear run on goal, but his shot ended in the arms of Edwin van der Sar.

A minute later, Okocha scuffed his effort wide after a through-ball from Frandsen.

The Nigerian playmaker then rattled the bar from a free kick after Ivan Campo had been hauled back by Davis.

Moritz Volz weaved his way into the penalty area on 39 minutes, but instead of squaring the ball across the face of goal, he went for the shot and was crowded out.

Bolton responded immediately, Campo heading just wide from a Youri Djorkaeff corner.

We took the lead shortly before the break, as an unmarked McBride headed home Luis Boa Morte's cross at the far post.

Henrik Pedersen set up Davies with a good delivery from the left on 62 minutes, but he couldn't get any power on the shot and van der Sar made an easy save.

McBride extended the lead in the 78th minute, steering a cross from Davis beyond Jaaskelainen.

Davies shot wide following a good cross from Pedersen as Bolton finished strongly.

"We fought hard, it wasn't always pretty and we were under a lot of pressure at times, but it was a good collective performance. Yet again, when we needed to pull out a result, we did. It's a credit to the lads." Chris Coleman

May Review

Month in Numbers

Games Played: **3**
Games Won: **1**
Games Drawn: **1**
Games Lost: **1**
Goals For: **3**
Goals Against: **2**

Results this Month

Premiership, 01/05/2004
Portsmouth 1-1 Fulham

Premiership, 09/05/2004
Fulham 0-1 Arsenal

Premiership, 15/05/2004
Bolton 0-2 Fulham

Premiership Table

Pos	(Apr)		Pl	W	D	L	F	A	Diff	Pts
1	(1)	Arsenal	38	26	12	0	73	26	+47	90
2	(2)	Chelsea	38	24	7	7	67	30	+37	79
3	(3)	Man Utd	38	23	6	9	64	35	+29	75
4	(4)	Liverpool	38	16	12	10	55	37	+18	60
5	(5)	Newcastle	38	13	17	8	52	40	+12	56
6	(6)	Aston Villa	38	15	11	12	48	44	+4	56
7	(8)	Charlton	38	14	11	13	51	51	0	53
8	(10)	Bolton	38	14	11	13	48	56	-8	53
9	**(7)**	**Fulham**	**38**	**14**	**10**	**14**	**52**	**46**	**+6**	**52**
10	(9)	Birmingham	38	12	14	12	43	48	-5	50
11	(12)	Middlesbro'	38	13	9	16	44	52	-8	48
12	(11)	Southampton	38	12	11	15	44	45	-1	47
13	(14)	Portsmouth	38	12	9	17	47	54	-7	45
14	(16)	Tottenham	38	13	6	19	47	57	-10	45
15	(13)	Blackburn	38	12	8	18	51	59	-8	44
16	(17)	Man City	38	9	14	15	55	54	+1	41
17	(15)	Everton	38	9	12	17	45	57	-12	39
18	(19)	Leicester	38	6	15	17	48	65	-17	33
19	(18)	Leeds	38	8	9	21	40	79	-39	33
20	(20)	Wolves	38	7	12	19	38	77	-39	33

Premiership Progression

Win:■ Draw:▨ Loss:■ League position: ❽ League position 2002-03: ⑧ Home fixtures in black

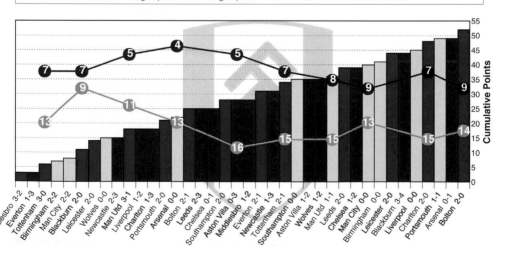

May Review

Premiership Performance

	May	03-04
Shots On Target	9	181
Shots Off Target	19	208
Hit Woodwork	1	9
Clean Sheets	1	15
Failed To Score	1	9
Caught Offside	4	88
Corners	12	157
Own Goals For	0	0
Own Goals Against	0	1

Goals Resulting From

	May		03-04	
	F	A	F	A
Open Play	3	1	39	29
Set Piece	0	1	13	16

How Goals Scored

	May		03-04	
	F	A	F	A
Right Foot	1	1	25	23
Left Foot	1	1	23	16
Header	1	0	4	6

When Goals Scored

	May		03-04	
	F	A	F	A
First Half	1	1	20	23
Second Half	2	1	32	22

Top Goal Scorers

	May	03-04
L. Saha	0	13
L. Boa Morte	0	9
S. Malbranque	0	6
S. Davis	0	5
C. John	0	4
B. McBride	3	4
B. Hayles	0	4

Top Goal Assists

	May	03-04
S. Malbranque	1	16
L. Boa Morte	1	8
L. Saha	0	5
S. Davis	1	4
L. Clark	0	4

Player of the Season

Edwin van der sar

The giant Dutchman picked up the Player of The Season award at the end of another consistently impressive campaign that saw him confirm his position as one of the best goalkeepers in the Premier League. A penalty save at Anfield and a clean sheet at Highbury - to deny the Champions elect from finding the back of the net for the first time in 47 games - were just two highlights from a magnificent year.

His hard work for the Whites was carried over in to Euro 2004 this summer for Holland as the Dutch Number One was named Goalkeeper of the Tournament by a whole host of pundits. A string of impressive saves including a remarkable reaction save against the Czech Republic and, of course, the Olof Mellberg penalty save that finally saw Holland break the penalty curse that had gripped them for their previous four international tournaments.

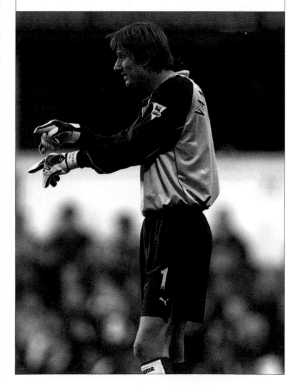

End of Season Review

Team Performance Table

League Position		Results (Home in caps)	Points Won (max. 6)	Points Won At Home (%)	Points Won Away (%)	Points Won Total (%)
1	Arsenal	dL	1			
2	Chelsea	Ll	-			
3	Man Utd	wD	4	7%	33%	20%
4	Liverpool	Ld	1			
5	Newcastle	Ll	-			
6	Aston Villa	lL	-			
7	Charlton	lW	3			
8	Bolton	Ww	6	58%	33%	46%
9	**Fulham**		**52**			
10	Birmingham	dD	2			
11	Middlesbrough	Wl	3			
12	Southampton	Wd	4			
13	Portsmouth	Wd	4	80%	53%	67%
14	Tottenham	wW	6			
15	Blackburn	wL	3			
16	Man City	Dd	2			
17	Everton	lW	3			
18	Leicester	Ww	6	73%	27%	50%
19	Leeds	lW	3			
20	Wolves	Dl	1			

Fulham's results against the other teams in the Premier League, along with how many points out of a possible six they have taken off each side. You can also see how many points they have taken from those available in each section as a percentage.

Season in Numbers

Total goals scored: **52**
Average Goals per Game: **1.3**
Fastest Goal (mins):
1 - Luis Boa Morte v Aston Villa (H)
Biggest League win: **3-0 v Tottenham (A)**

Squad List 2003-04

		League Appearances	Appearances as Sub	Goals/Clean Sheets	Assists	Yellow Cards	Red Cards
G	M.Crossley	1					
G	E.van der Sar	37	15				
D	C.Bocanegra	15				2	1
D	J.Bonnissel	16			1		
D	A.Goma	23				5	
D	A.Green	4				1	
D	J.Harley	3	1				
D	Z.Knight	30	1		1	4	
D	D.Leacock	3	1			2	
D	A.Melville	9					
D	I.Pearce	12	1		1		
D	M.Volz	32	1			5	
M	L.Boa Morte	32	1	9	8	9	1
M	M.Buari	1	2				
M	L.Clark	25		2	4	2	
M	S.Davis	22	2	5	4	5	
M	M.Djetou	19	7			3	
M	J.Inamoto	15	7	2	1	8	
M	S.Legwinski	30	2		2	7	1
M	S.Malbranque	38		6	16	3	
M	M.Pembridge	9	3	1		1	
M	B.Petta	3	6				
M	Z.Rehman		1				
F	B.Hayles	10	16	4	3	2	
F	C.John	3	5	4	1	1	
F	S.Marlet	1	1				
F	B.McBride	5	11	4	1		
F	D.Pratley		1				
F	L.Saha	20	1	13	5	1	
F	F.Sava		6	1			

Premier League Results Table 2003-04

Date		H-T	F/T	Pos	van der Sar	Volz	Goma	Djetou	Bonnissel	Marlet	Legwinski	Inamoto	Clark	Malbranque	Saha	Subs
6/08	H Middlesbrough	1-1	3-2	3	van der Sar	Volz	Goma	Djetou ▲	Bonnissel	Marlet 18 ●	Legwinski ●	Inamoto 56	Clark	Malbranque 70	Saha 18 56 70 ▲	Hayles ▲ Boa Morte ▲
23/08	A Everton	0-3	1-3	11	van der Sar	Volz ●	Goma ●	Knight	Bonnissel	Malbranque ●	Legwinski	Inamoto ▲	Clark	Boa Morte	Saha 69	Hayles ▲●69 Knight ▲ Buari ▲
30/08	A Tottenham	1-1	3-0	7	van der Sar	Volz ●	Goma ●	Knight	Bonnissel	Malbranque 67	Legwinski	Inamoto ●	Clark	Boa Morte 71	Hayles 23 67 71 ▲	Saha ▲ Pembridge ▲ Djetou ▲
14/09	A Birmingham	1-1	2-2	9	van der Sar	Volz	Goma ●	Knight	Bonnissel 1	Malbranque ●	Legwinski	Inamoto ●	Clark 23	Boa Morte 78 ●	Saha 1 ▲	Pembridge ▲ Sava ▲
20/09	H Man City	0-0	2-2	10	van der Sar	Volz	Goma	Knight	Bonnissel	Malbranque 73 79	Legwinski	Inamoto ●	Clark 78	Boa Morte 72 ▲	Saha 79	Pembridge ▲
28/09	A Blackburn	1-0	2-0	7	van der Sar	Volz ▲	Goma	Knight ●	Bonnissel ●	Malbranque 5	Pembridge	Inamoto ● 56	Clark ●	Boa Morte 5 ●▲	Saha 56	Leacock ▲● Buari ▲
04/10	H Leicester	1-0	2-0	4	van der Sar	Leacock ▲	Goma ▲	Knight ●	Bonnissel ●	Malbranque 36 73	Pembridge	Inamoto ●▲	Clark	Boa Morte 36 73	Saha ▲	Legwinski ▲ Djetou ▲ Hayles ▲
18/10	H Wolves	0-0	0-0	5	van der Sar	Leacock ●	Goma ●	Knight	Bonnissel	Malbranque	Pembridge	Inamoto ●▲	Clark 5	Boa Morte	Saha ▲	Hayles ▲
21/10	H Newcastle	2-1	2-3	6	van der Sar	Leacock	Goma	Knight	Bonnissel	Malbranque 5	Pembridge ▲	Buari ▲	Clark 3	Legwinski 7 ●	Saha 7	Inamoto ▲
25/10	A Man Utd	1-1	3-1	7	van der Sar	Volz	Goma	Knight ●	Bonnissel ▲	Malbranque 3 66 79	Pembridge ▲	Legwinski	Clark	Boa Morte	Saha 66	Inamoto ▲79 Djetou ▲ Hayles ▲
02/11	H Liverpool	1-1	1-2	6	van der Sar	Volz	Melville	Knight	Bonnissel ▲	Pembridge ▲	Pembridge ▲	Legwinski	Clark	Boa Morte ●●	Saha 40 ▲	Djetou ▲ Hayles ▲
08/11	A Charlton	0-1	1-3	7	van der Sar	Volz	Melville	Knight	Bonnissel	Inamoto ●▲	Clark	Legwinski ●	Boa Morte ●89	Boa Morte	Saha ▲	Hayles ▲ Davis S ▲ 89 Pratley ▲
24/11	H Portsmouth	2-0	2-0	5	van der Sar	Volz	Melville	Knight	Bonnissel	Malbranque	Malbranque	Legwinski ●	Clark 33	Boa Morte	Saha 30 33 ▲	Inamoto ▲ Sava ▲
30/11	A Arsenal	0-0	0-0	4	van der Sar	Volz	Melville	Knight	Bonnissel	Inamoto	Davis S	Legwinski	Clark	Boa Morte	Saha ▲	Hayles ▲
06/12	H Bolton	0-2	1-0	4	van der Sar	Volz ▲	Melville	Knight	Harley	Inamoto ▲	Davis S 75 ▲	Legwinski	Clark	Boa Morte 63	Saha ▲	Hayles ▲75 76 Sava ▲ 76 Djetou ▲
14/12	A Leeds Utd	0-1	2-3	4	van der Sar	Volz	Melville	Knight	Harley	Malbranque 86	Davis S 47	Legwinski	Boa Morte	Boa Morte ●▲	Saha 47 86	Hayles ▲ Sava ▲
20/12	H Chelsea	0-0	0-1	4	van der Sar	Volz	Melville	Knight	Green	Malbranque	Davis S ▲	Legwinski ▲	Clark ●	Boa Morte	Saha ▲	Djetou ▲ Sava ▲
26/12	A Southampton	1-0	0-4	4	van der Sar	Djetou ▲	Goma	Knight	Green	Malbranque ▲	Inamoto	Djetou	Clark	Boa Morte	Saha 19 63	Harley ▲
28/12	A Aston Villa	0-1	0-3	5	van der Sar	Volz	Goma	Knight	Bonnissel ▲	Malbranque	Inamoto ▲	Legwinski ▲	Clark	Boa Morte	Saha ▲	Hayles ▲ Sava ▲
07/01	H Middlesbrough	0-1	1-2	7	van der Sar ●	Djetou ▲	Goma	Knight	Harley	Malbranque 45 46	Davis S ● 90	Legwinski ▲	Clark	Boa Morte 45 ▲	Saha ▲	Hayles ▲ 90 Petta ▲
10/01	H Everton	0-2	1-3	7	van der Sar	Volz ●	Melville	Knight	Green	Malbranque 45	Davis S	Legwinski ▲	Clark	Boa Morte ●	Saha	Petta ▲
19/01	A Newcastle	1-1	2-1	6	van der Sar	Volz	Melville	Knight	Green	Malbranque	Davis S 74	Legwinski ▲	Clark ▲	Boa Morte 45 ▲	Saha 45 46	Volz ▲ Sava ▲
31/01	H Tottenham	0-0	0-0	7	van der Sar	Volz	Pearce 67	Knight	Bocanegra	Malbranque ●	Davis S ●	Djetou ▲	Clark ▲	Hayles ●▲	Hayles ● ▲	McBride ▲ 67 Petta ▲ Legwinski ▲
07/02	A Southampton	0-0	0-0	7	van der Sar ●	Volz ●	Pearce	Knight	Bocanegra	Malbranque	Davis S	Legwinski ▲	Clark 1 ▲	McBride	McBride	Petta ▲ Hayles ▲
11/02	H Aston Villa	1-2	1-2	8	van der Sar	Volz	Pearce	Knight ●	Bocanegra ●	Malbranque 84	Davis S ●	Djetou ▲	Clark 1 ▲	Boa Morte 1	McBride	Petta ▲ Djetou ▲
21-02	A Wolves	0-1	1-1	8	van der Sar	Volz	Pearce	Knight ▲	Bocanegra	Malbranque	Davis S	Legwinski	Boa Morte 84	McBride	Petta ▲	Petta ▲ Inamoto ▲
28/02	H Man Utd	0-0	2-0	8	van der Sar	Volz	Pearce	Knight 83	Green	Malbranque 71	Davis S 71	Legwinski ●	Petta ▲	McBride 64	McBride	Boa Morte 64 McBride ▲
13/03	H Leeds Utd	0-0	2-1	8	van der Sar ●	Volz ●	Goma	Knight 83	Green ●	Malbranque	Davis S 19	Djetou ●	Pembridge 19 ▲	Boa Morte 83 ●	McBride	Hayles ▲ McBride ▲
20/03	A Chelsea	1-2	1-2	9	van der Sar	Volz	Pearce	Knight	Bocanegra	Malbranque	Davis S ●	Djetou ●▲	Pembridge 19 ▲	Hayles ▲	McBride ▲	Hayles ▲ McBride ▲
27/03	A Man City	0-0	0-0	9	van der Sar	Volz	Goma	Knight	Bocanegra	Malbranque	Davis S	Djetou	Pembridge	Boa Morte	McBride ▲	Hayles ▲ McBride ▲
03/04	H Birmingham	0-0	0-0	10	van der Sar	Volz	Goma	Knight	Bocanegra ●▲	Malbranque	Davis S ●	Djetou ▲	Legwinski	Hayles ▲	Hayles ▲	McBride ▲ Pearce ▲
10/04	A Leicester	0-0	2-0	8	van der Sar	Volz	Goma	Knight	Bocanegra	Malbranque 66 ▲	Legwinski	Djetou	Legwinski	Boa Morte 89	John 66 89	John ▲ 66 89 Hayles ▲ McBride ▲
12/04	A Blackburn	2-1	3-4	10	van der Sar	Volz	Goma	Knight	Bocanegra ▲	Malbranque 26 45 ▲	Davis S ▲	Djetou	Legwinski	Boa Morte 60	John 26 45 60 ▲	Petta ▲ McBride ▲ Hayles ▲
17/04	H Liverpool	1-0	2-0	10	van der Sar ●	Volz ●	Pearce	Goma	Bocanegra ●	Malbranque 18	Legwinski	Djetou ▲	Petta ▲	Boa Morte	McBride ▲	John 26 45 60 ▲ McBride ▲ McBride ▲
24/04	A Charlton	0-0	1-0	7	van der Sar	Volz	Pearce	Goma	Bocanegra ●	Malbranque 18	Legwinski	Djetou ▲	Petta ▲	Boa Morte 18 64 ▲	Davis S ▲ 64	Davis S ▲ 64 McBride ▲ Rehman ▲
01/05	A Portsmouth	0-0	1-1	9	van der Sar	Volz	Pearce	Goma	Bocanegra	Inamoto	Davis S 85	Djetou ▲	Legwinski	Boa Morte	McBride ▲ 85	Boa Morte 18 64 ▲ Davis S ▲ 64 McBride ▲
09/05	H Arsenal	0-1	0-1	9	van der Sar	Volz	Pearce	Goma	Bocanegra	Davis S ●	Legwinski	Djetou ▲	Legwinski	Boa Morte	McBride ▲	McBride ▲ 85 John ▲ John ▲
15/05	A Bolton	1-0	2-0	9	van der Sar	Volz	Pearce	Goma	Bocanegra	Malbranque 78	Davis S	Djetou	Legwinski	Boa Morte 45 ●	McBride 45 78 ▲	Boa Morte 45 ● 78 ▲ John ▲

Key: 88 Time of goal 88 Time of assist ▲ Player substituted ● Yellow card ● Red card

Fulham Reserves
End of Season Review

Fixtures and Results 2003-04

Premier Reserve League (Southern)

August 2003

Wed 13	Derby County (A)	D	5-5
Wed 20	Nottingham F (H)	D	0-0
Tue 26	Tottenham (A)	W	2-1

September 2003

Wed 3	Wimbledon (H)	W	1-0
Tue 9	Charlton (A)	L	0-4
Mon 22	Southampton (H)	L	1-3
Tue 30	Portsmouth (A)	D	1-1

October 2003

Wed 8	Watford (A)	D	2-2
Tue 14	Leicester City (A)	L	0-3
Mon 20	Arsenal (A)	D	1-1
Wed 29	West Ham (H)	W	1-0

November 2003

Mon 3	Chelsea (A)	L	0-1
Wed 12	Ipswich (H)	L	1-6
Tue 18	Coventry City (A)	L	0-4

December 2003

| Wed 3 | Charlton (H) | D | 1-1 |
| Wed 10 | Portsmouth (H) | W | 2-1 |

January 2004

Tue 13	Southampton (A)	L	0-3
Wed 21	Derby County (H)	L	0-2
Tue 27	Nottingham F (A)	D	1-1

February 2004

Tue 3	Tottenham (H)	W	1-0
Tue 10	Wimbledon (A)	L	1-2
Wed 18	Leicester City (H)	W	2-0
Wed 25	Watford (H)	L	2-4

March 2004

| Tue 9 | Arsenal (H) | L | 1-3 |
| Tue 23 | West Ham (A) | L | 0-1 |

April 2004

Wed 7	Chelsea (H)	L	0-3
Wed 14	Ipswich (A)	L	0-1
Wed 21	Coventry City (H)	D	1-1

Premier Reserve League (Southern Section) 2003-04

Pos		Pl	W	D	L	F	A	Diff	Pts
1	Charlton Athletic	28	17	6	5	46	19	27	57
2	Derby County	28	13	10	5	46	35	15	49
3	Southampton	28	14	6	8	43	28	15	48
4	West Ham United	28	12	8	8	37	35	2	44
5	Tottenham Hotspur	28	11	9	8	42	30	7	42
6	Arsenal	28	10	9	9	41	38	6	39
7	Chelsea	28	11	6	8	37	33	4	39
8	Leicester City	28	9	11	8	34	40	-6	38
9	Coventry City	28	9	10	9	38	40	-2	37
10	Wimbledon	28	9	5	14	35	47	-12	32
11	Watford	28	6	12	10	32	40	-8	30
12	Portsmouth	28	6	11	11	36	39	-3	29
13	Nottingham Forest	28	6	11	11	33	41	-8	29
14	Ipswich Town	28	8	4	16	34	44	-10	28
15	**Fulham**	**28**	**6**	**8**	**14**	**27**	**54**	**-27**	**26**

Reserve Squad List

Player	Apps	Goals
Nik Baker	1	-
Dave Beasant	7	-
Luis Boa Morte	1	-
Malik Buari	22	2
Matt Collins	0+2	-
Mark Crossley	5	-
Sean Davis	4	1
Tom Davis	14+6	2
Martin Djetou	2	-
Sean Doherty	14+4	-
Loui Fazakerley	10+10	1
Ross Flitney	14	-
Liam Fontaine	17+1	-
Alain Goma	0+1	-
Adam Green	18+2	1
Elvis Hammond	1+1	-
Jon Harley	8	-
Barry Hayles	2	-
Mark Hudson	2	-
Junichi Inamoto	3	-
Chris James	2+3	-
Collins John	2	1
Zat Knight	2	-
Ismael Kouadio	1+4	1
Alex Lawless	0+3	-
Dean Leacock	12	-
Neale McDermott	6+9	2
William McFrederick	1	-
Andy Melville	3	-
Robert Milsom	2	-
Stuart Noble	20+4	4
Ian Pearce	1	-
Mark Pembridge	3	-
Bobby Petta	2	-
Darren Pratley	22	-
Zesh Rehman	16	1
Liam Rosenior	19+1	1
Facundo Sava	12	6
Andrejs Stolcers	11+3	3
Daniel Stratford	8+5	-
Robert Watkins	15+1	-
Danny White	1	-
Calum Willock	2+2	-
Opponent o.g	-	1

Fulham Academy
End of Season Review

The Under 17s

2003/04 was a challenging and fulfilling season for the Under 17s as the young team came up against older, more experienced teams and played admirably throughout.

With the majority of the Academy players playing above their age group throughout the season the U17s consisted of many players who would normally fall in to the U16s. It was therefore a story of experience and development for this exciting crop of youngsters.

Before the Academy season even kicked off the U17s played a number of teams from Centre of Excellence programmes and gained some good results. Once underway, however, the season was hard and the players had to learn fast as they came up against some tough opponents.

Having said this the U17s competed well against some very strong teams including Southampton and Aston Villa. Maturing all the time the team put in a strong performance up at Liverpool where they displayed a very high standard of football.

It was a difficult test for the players physically, mentally and even socially but, after Christmas, the benefits of playing the boys up a level became clear. The team bonded together well, adjusted to the pace of the games and technically and tactically it was clear that they had improved. In short, things certainly got better and better as the season progressed.

Under 17s: Final League Table

Pos		Pl	W	D	L	F	A	Diff	Pts
1	Aston Villa	26	16	5	5	90	41	+49	53
2	Leicester City	26	14	5	7	59	54	+5	47
3	Coventry	26	12	6	8	55	46	+9	42
4	Arsenal	26	12	6	8	39	40	-1	42
5	Birmingham	26	11	7	8	52	47	+5	40
6	Bristol City	26	9	3	14	55	62	-7	30
7	**Fulham**	**26**	**7**	**6**	**13**	**37**	**56**	**-19**	**27**
8	Watford	26	5	5	16	38	71	-33	20

The Under 19s

Just as with the Under 17s, last season's Under 19 team included many young players who – despite playing above their age group – had a hugely successful season.

Stating their case for being the possible stars of Fulham's future the Under 19 team consisted of a number of young players who took a step up after the side lost several key players to Paul Nevin's Reserve side.

These young players, however, more than rose to the challenge and developed considerably as the season went on. Often playing against much more experienced sides the players may well have found it difficult to compete at times but that was purely due to physical differences. Their willingness to learn and obvious progress over the course of the campaign pleased all the Academy coaches.

Amongst the list of Under 19 representatives who did well throughout 2003/04 were Ismael Ehui, Chris James, Mark Davidson, Robert Milsom, Liam Fontaine, Robert Watkins, Matt Collins, Michael Timlin, Alex Lawless, Nik Baker, Neale McDermott, Nik Bagley and Calum Legate.

Under 19s: Final League Table

Pos		Pl	W	D	L	F	A	Diff	Pts
1	Arsenal	26	16	4	6	58	29	+29	52
2	Chelsea	26	12	3	11	40	33	+7	39
3	Aston Villa	26	12	2	12	54	48	+6	38
4	Birmingham	26	10	7	9	30	24	+6	37
5	Leicester City	26	10	5	11	40	43	-3	35
6	Watford	26	10	5	11	38	51	-13	35
7	Reading	26	9	4	13	36	40	-4	31
8	**Fulham**	**26**	**4**	**7**	**15**	**22**	**52**	**-30**	**19**
9	Bristol City	26	3	5	18	37	64	-27	14

Fulham Ladies
End of Season Review

Fixtures and Results 2003-04

August 2003			
Wed 6	Derby County (A)	D	5-5
Sun 31	Nottingham F (H)	D	0-0

September 2003			
Sun 7	Tottenham (A)	W	2-1
Sun 14	Wimbledon (H)	W	1-0
Wed 17	Charlton (A)	L	0-4
Sun 21	Southampton (H)	L	1-3
Sun 28	Portsmouth (A)	D	1-1

October 2003			
Sun 5	Watford (A)	D	2-2
Sun 12	Leicester City (A)	L	0-3
Wed 15	Arsenal (A)	D	1-1
Sun 26	West Ham (H)	W	1-0

November 2003			
Sun 2	Chelsea (A)	L	0-1
Sun 9	Ipswich (H)	L	1-6
Sun 16	Coventry City (A)	L	0-4
Sun 30	Charlton (H)	D	1-1

December 2003			
Sun 7	Portsmouth (H)	W	2-1
Sun 14	Southampton (A)	L	0-3

January 2004			
Sun 4	Derby County (H)	L	0-2
Sun 18	Nottingham F (A)	D	1-1
Sun 25	Tottenham (H)	W	1-0

February 2004			
Sun 8	Wimbledon (A)	L	1-2
Sun 15	Leicester City (H)	W	2-0
Sun 22	Watford (H)	L	2-4
Sun 29	Arsenal (H)	L	1-3

March 2004			
Sun 7	West Ham (A)	L	0-1
Sun 14	Chelsea (H)	L	0-3
Sun 28	Ipswich (A)	L	0-1

April 2004			
Sun 18	Coventry City (H)	D	1-1

May 2004			
Sun 2	Coventry City (H)	D	1-1
Sat 15	Coventry City (H)	D	1-1

Fulham Ladies
End of Season Review

Last season saw many changes at Fulham Ladies. Ex-England International Marieanne Spacey took the managerial reins, the teams status changed to semi-professional, players left and many new faces arrived. Despite the changes and a side relatively inexperienced in playing together Fulham Ladies had a very successful season. They won the Community Shield, achieved a Quarter Final place in the UEFA Cup, reached the Final of the League Cup and took the Championship race to an end of season play-off with Arsenal.

This was one of the closest title run-ins in history and was an excellent advertisement for the game. Infront of the Sky cameras and over 5000 fans at Highbury Fulham played Arsenal in a game which both sides had to win to lift the title, a draw would have gifted Charlton Athletic the Cup. Arsenal won but all three teams have received plaudits for their consistency and professionalism throughout the season.

The only English side to compete in the UEFA Women's European Cup Fulham Ladies won the qualifying group, winning all three games, scoring 20 goals and conceding only two. In an exciting two leg Quarter Final Fulham Ladies were beaten by formidable German side FFC Frankfurt but the experience was fantastic for players and staff alike.

In the League Cup the girls beat Birmingham, Langford, Leeds and Bristol City to progress to the Final where they were narrowly beaten by Charlton Athletic. Charlton were also successful in knocking Fulham out of the FA Cup but were eventually beaten by Arsenal in the Final.

Marieanne Spacey is probably the most famous name in womens football in the UK. She has over 91 caps, has played in seven European Championships and - during her ten year career with Arsenal - won no less than four Premier League titles, four FA Cups and five Premier League Cups.

However, Fulham Ladies Football Club is not just about the First Team - growing the game at grass-roots is equally as important. The Club has a Centre of Excellence for girls from the age of 10 −16, has recently opened an Academy at a local college to encourage young women to continue playing whilst undertaking higher education and it also runs girls-only soccer coaching through seven Boroughs in London and Surrey.

Womens football is very much a family affair; it attracts a wide audience of men, women and children. Fulham Ladies train and play all their home games at the Club's Motspur Park Training Ground. Games are generally played on a Sunday afternoon with a 2pm kick off. Tickets cost just £3 for adults and £1 for children.

FA Nationwide Women's Premier League National Division									
Pos		Pl	W	D	L	F	A	Diff	Pts
1	Arsenal LFC	18	15	2	1	65	11	+54	47
2	Charlton A. WFC	18	15	1	2	52	17	+35	46
3	**Fulham LFC**	**18**	**14**	**2**	**2**	**60**	**20**	**+40**	**44**
4	Leeds United	18	8	4	6	32	28	+4	28
5	Doncaster R. Belles	18	8	3	7	41	40	+1	27
6	Everton LFC	18	6	2	10	21	36	-15	20
7	Birmingham C. LFC	18	4	5	9	17	31	-14	17
8	Bristol Rovers WFC	18	3	3	12	27	37	-10	12
9	Aston Villa LFC	18	1	4	13	18	63	-45	7
10	Tranmere R. LFC	18	1	4	13	13	63	-50	7

Luis
Boa Morte

Personal Information

Position: Striker / Midfield
Date of Birth: 04/08/77
Weight: 72.34kg
Height: 178cm
Place of Birth: Lisbon, Portugal
Fee: £1.7m
Previous Clubs: Sporting Lisbon, Arsenal, Southampton
Debut: Crewe (H) 12/08/00

Biography

Luis Boa Morte was signed by Arsenal in 1997 after Arsene Wenger had watched him represent Portugal in a friendly Under 21 tournament. However, with such tough competition for a regular place at Highbury, David Jones took Luis to Southampton where the prospect of regular football was a more realistic. However Glenn Hoddle's arrival on the South Coast saw Luis once again spending more time on the bench.

However, Jean Tigana saw enough talent in the forward to bring him for a trial at Fulham. A year-long loan deal followed as Luis took his place amongst a strike force that would come to terrorize the First Division. He scored 21 goals in Fulham's Championship-winning campaign, including the memorable goal away at Huddersfield Town that saw the Whites clinch promotion to the Premiership.

He was rewarded for his remarkable season by receiving his international call up for Portugal, and by making his move to Fulham permanent, signing a four year deal for £1.7million in summer 2001.

Since Fulham's arrival in the Premiership, Boa has reverted to his preferred position as an attacking left-sided midfielder. He has continued to appear for his country but narrowly missed out on making the Portugal squad for Euro 2004.

Last season Boa ended the campaign as the Club's second highest goalscorer, netting ten 10 during 2003/04.

Carlos
Bocanegra

Personal Information

Position: Defence
Date of Birth: 25/05/79
Weight: 78kg
Height: 182cm
Place of Birth: California, USA
Fee: Undisclosed
Previous Clubs: Chicago Fire
Debut: Newcastle (A) 19/01/04

Biography

With Jerome Bonnissel injured before Christmas Chris Coleman was left with a defensive headache prior to the January 2004 transfer window. However, the arrival of American international Carlos Bocanegra, from MLS side Chicago Fire, provided a worthy solution with the young American stepping into the vacant position.

Despite being a central defender by trade, Bocanegra proved a more than capable of deputising as a full back, took to life in the Premiership with ease and quickly established himself as a regular in the side. Carlos has also become a regular in the US national side over the last two seasons.

Jerome
Bonnissel

Personal Information

Position: Defence
Date of Birth: 11/04/73
Weight: 70.2kg
Height: 175.3cm
Place of Birth: Montpellier, France
Previous Clubs: Montpellier, Deportivo La Coruna,
Bordeaux, Rangers (loan)
Fee: Free
Debut: Middlesbrough (H) 16/08/03

Biography

**31-year-old French left-sided defender Jerome
Bonnissel was born in Montpellier and began
his professional career with his home town
club where he played from 1992-96.**

At the end of the 1995/96 season Bonnissel
moved to Spain where he joined Deportivo La Coruna.
The Frenchman made 63 appearances for the La Liga
side before moving back home to France and to
Bordeaux in July 1999.

Bonnissel was with Bordeaux for three years
before moving to Glasgow Rangers on loan during the
January 2003 transfer window. He made a handful of
appearances for the Scottish Champions before being
released at the end of the season. Bonnissel
participated in Fulham's pre-season training camp in
Austria in summer 2003 before signing a permanent
contract on his return and was widely viewed as the
bargain signing of summer 2003.

Jerome played an important part in Chris
Coleman's side for the first half of the last campaign
before an ankle injury ended his season in December.
However, following surgery and a lengthy rehabilitation
process Bonnissel will be eager to regain his place in
the starting eleven in 2004/05.

Malik
Buari

Personal Information

Position: Midfield
Date of Birth: 24/04/84
Weight: 75.2kg
Height: 181.2cm
Place of Birth: Accra, Ghana
Previous Clubs: Fulham Academy
Debut: Wigan (A) 23/09/03

Biography

A right-sided midfielder with an eye for goal Malik scored twice for the Reserves and made four appearances for the First Team, including one start against Newcastle at Loftus Road in October.

A vital part of Paul Nevin's Reserve side he provided much attacking force to the team and caused opposing defenders all sorts of problems throughout the season.

Lee
Clark

Personal Information

Position: Midfield
Date of Birth: 27/10/72
Weight: 73kg
Height: 172cm
Place of Birth: Wallsend
Fee: £3m
Previous Clubs: Newcastle Utd, Sunderland
Debut: Birmingham City (A) 07/08/99

Biography

Dynamic midfielder Lee Clark broke the Club's transfer record when he signed from Sunderland for £3 million in July 1999.

Named as the Club's Player of the Year in his first season at Fulham, Clark's career started at his beloved Newcastle United, where he spent eight formative years. His move to Sunderland in 1997 came as a surprise but Clark's desire for regular first team football superceded any allegiances as a fan.

Despite playing a vital part in Fulham's 2000/01 Championship-winning campaign, Clark had a bitterly disappointing first Premiership season with Fulham with a persistent Achilles injury keeping him on the sidelines.

Having regained his fitness, Clark was hugely unlucky the following season when he was struck down by an almost identical injury to his opposite calf. However, hard work and persistence saw him back in time to play a crucial role in Fulham's relegation battle at the end of 2002/03.

Ever-present in the side for the first half of Chris Coleman's inaugural season, Clark also assumed the mantle of Club Captain following Andy Melville's departure in January 2004. However he was once again sidelined by injury for the majority of the second half of the season but regained fitness during the summer and will be keen to make up for lost time during 2004/05.

Mark
Crossley

Personal Information

Position: Goalkeeper
Date of Birth: 16/04/69
Weight: 95.8kg
Height: 183cm
Place of Birth: Barnsley
Fee: Undisclosed
Previous Clubs: Notts Forest, Middlesbrough
Debut: Wigan (A) 23/09/03

Biography

Signed in summer 2003 to replace Maik Taylor, Crossley brings a wealth of experience to the Fulham side. Mark began his career with Nottingham Forest for whom he made over 370 appearances between 1987 and 2000.

Following loan spells with Manchester United and Millwall, Crossley then signed for Middlesbrough in July 2000. However, the presence of Mark Schwarzer restricted his appearances with the Teesiders, resulting in two consecutive loan spells with Stoke City.

A Welsh international, Crossley is well known by Chris Coleman and has been a key part of the squad despite playing second fiddle to Edwin van der Sar. The Dutchman's impressive form in 2003/04 restricted Crossley to a solitary Premiership outing. However, as expected, his display against Liverpool at Loftus Road certainly revealed his unquestionable pedigree.

Martin
Djetou

Position: Defence / Midfield
Date of Birth: 15/12/74
Weight: 79kg
Height: 180cm
Place of Birth: Brogohio, France
Fee: On loan from Parma
Previous Clubs: Strasbourg, Monaco, Parma
Debut: West Ham 23/10/02

Biography

In July 2002 Fulham announced the loan signing of French International Martin Djetou from Italian club Parma. Djetou, born in the Ivory Coast, spent four seasons with RC Strasbourg before joining Monaco in 1996 where, under Jean Tigana, he helped his side win the French Championship in his first season at the club.

Despite being linked with Fulham in summer 2001 Djetou made a £6.5m move from Monaco to Serie A club Parma and formed part of the squad that prevented Juventus from winning the double by defeating them in the Final of the Coppa Italia.

The 29-year-old has six international caps for France making his first appearance for the national side in the 4-0 win against Turkey in October 1996. A versatile player, Djetou can play as a centre-half, a right back, or in front of the back four.

At the time of going to print his future at the club was uncertain.

Alain
Goma

Personal Information

Position: Defender
Date of Birth: 05/10/72
Weight: 86kg
Height: 183cm
Place of Birth: Sault, France
Fee: £4m
Previous Clubs: Auxerre, PSG, Newcastle
Debut: Portsmouth (A) 21/04/01

Biography

**Alain's career in professional football began
at the academy of AJ Auxerre in 1988.
He made his League debut in 1991and a year
later was selected for the French Under 21
side. In 1994, Goma and his Auxerre team
mates won the French FA Cup which also lead
to a UEFA Cup place.**

Goma made over 200 appearances in a 10 year
spell with Auxerre before moving to French giants
Paris St Germain, where he made 30 appearances
and won the Champion's Trophy (French equivalent
of the Charity Shield). In 1999 Goma joined
Newcastle United where he became an integral
part of the Magpies' defence.

Goma broke Fulham's transfer record in March
2001 when he signed for £4 million (breaking the
previous record of £3 million paid to Sunderland for
Lee Clark) and worked hard to regain his fitness
during that summer after a season of persistent
injuries.

Since his arrival is West London his composed
and elegant style has seen him become a stalwart
figure in the centre of the Fulham defence, hence his
nickname, "The Rock."

Adam
Green

Personal Information

Position: Defence
Date of Birth: 12/01/84
Weight: 67.6kg
Height: 176.2cm
Place of Birth: Hillingdon
Fee: N/A
Previous Clubs: Fulham Academy
Debut: Wigan (A) 23/09/03

Biography

Playing against Manchester United is daunting enough for any professional footballer but, for a 20-year-old Academy graduate, the opportunity face the biggest team in the world twice in a week is a dream come true.

Young left back Adam Green did just that last season and in a total of seven starts he proved his potential against some of the best forwards in the Premiership.

An attacking full-back with surprising strength and natural skill, Adam is every bit the Premiership star in the making and signed a new contract in summer 2004 that will keep him at the Club until the June 2006.

Elvis
Hammond

Position: Striker
Date of Birth: 06/10/80
Weight: 76.5kg
Height: 181cm
Place of Birth: Accra, Ghana
Fee: N/A
Previous Clubs: Fulham Academy
Debut: Chesterfield (A) 19/09/00

Biography

Elvis joined Fulham's Academy at Under 16 level and has been a persistent goal scorer in the years since. However, despite breaking in to the First Team at the tail end of the 2002/03 season (during which he was top goalscorer in the Premier Reserve League South with 13 goals) an injury stricken 2003/04 meant that he largely watched from the sidelines.

A powerful and pacey striker with a natural eye for goal his Fulham First Team debut came in 2000/01 when he appeared as a substitute in the League Cup game at Chesterfield. Elvis has dual nationality after being born in Ghana to a British mother and has played with some of the big Ghanaian names such as Marcel Desailly, George Weah, Roger Milla and Abedi Pele.

Having worked hard last season to regain his match fitness, and following a short loan spell at Norwich City, Elvis will undoubtedly be looking to reaffirm his potential as a regular Premiership striker this season.

Junichi
Inamoto

Personal Information

Position: Midfield
Date of Birth: 18/09/79
Weight: 75kg
Height: 181cm
Place of Birth: Osaka, Japan
Fee: On loan
Previous Clubs: Gamba Osaka, Arsenal (loan)
Debut: Sochaux (H) 31/07/02

Biography

Following much media speculation after the 2002 World Cup, Fulham announced the signing of Japanese international Junichi Inamoto in July 2002. "Ina" arrived from Arsenal where he was on loan from Japanese club Gamba Osaka for the 2001/02 season.

Ina became the first Japanese player to transfer to an English club when he signed for Arsenal in July 2001. One of the stars of the Japanese national team, the 24-year-old midfielder blossomed in the 2002 World Cup. His 67th minute strike against Belgium helped earn Japan their first World Cup point and a Budweiser Man of the Match Award came his way in return. A few days later in Yokohama Ina grabbed the headlines again scoring the only goal in Japan's 1-0 defeat of the Russians.

A tenacious, all action central midfielder with an impressive work rate, Ina scored the hat-trick that secured the InterToto Cup for Fulham in 2002 and with it, a place in the 2002/03 UEFA Cup.

At the time of going to print his future at Fulham was still undecided.

Collins
John

Personal Information

Position: Striker
Date of Birth: 07/10/85
Weight: 82kg
Height: 181cm
Place of Birth: Zwandru, Liberia
Fee: Undisclosed
Previous Clubs: FC Twente
Debut: Chelsea (A) 20/03/04

Biography

A star in the making Collins scored four times in his first eight appearances for the Whites at the tail end of 2003/04. Two braces against Leicester and Blackburn showed what huge potential the Liberian born Dutch international has and, at just 18, his future is looking incredibly bright.

Having previously played in the Dutch league Collins left former club FC Twente as leading scorer and, in the January 2004 transfer window, completed a dream move to the Premiership.

Once he had recovered from an injury sustained prior to his move the youngster – who has played at almost every junior level for Holland – wasted no time in staking his claim for a spot in the starting eleven. His only regret being that his injury prevented him from getting on the scoresheet earlier.

Zat
Knight

Personal Information

Position: Defence
Date of Birth: 02/05/80
Weight: 89kg
Height: 198.1cm
Place of Birth: Solihull
Fee: Free
Previous Clubs: Rushall Olympic
Debut: Northampton (H) 05/09/00

Biography

Kevin Keegan signed Zat after the youngster returned from a trial period with Portuguese giants, Benfica. A strikingly tall player with two good feet, Zat has progressed well since first joining the Club.

A strong central defender with obvious natural skill, Zat was immediately recognised as a talented prospect by Jean Tigana, under whose guidance he made a number of promising performances during Fulham's first season in the Premier League.

During 2002/03 Zat's appearances continued to increase however, it was Chris Coleman who gave Zat his big chance by making him an almost ever present at the heart of the Fulham defence last season. His consistently impressive performances also caught the eye of Sven Goran Eriksson who admitted that the giant defender could feature in his plans at some stage.

However, playing for England – when the time eventually comes – will not be a new experience for Zat who, together with Sean Davis, played in the 2002 European Under 21 Championships in Switzerland.

Dean
Leacock

Personal Information

Position: Centre back / Right back
Date of Birth: 10/06/84
Weight: 78kg
Height: 189cm
Place of Birth: Croydon
Fee: N/A
Previous Clubs: Fulham Academy
Debut: Wigan (A) 04/12/02

Biography

Dean is a quick, strong defender with good technique and excellent distribution. He can occupy either a full back or a centre half role. A local boy, who originally hails from Thornton Heath, he made his debut for Fulham two seasons ago in a Fourth Round Worthington Cup game away at Wigan.

Predominantly right footed, Dean also has a useful left foot and is an expert at long diagonal passes.

Last season Dean was a contender for the Young Player of The Season Award despite suffering a frustrating knee injury which limited his involvement. He played at right back in three successive Premiership home games - against Leicester City, Wolves and Newcastle - impressing in all. In a total of four starts last season, as well as a number of Reserve appearances, the 20-year-old has shown himself to be an exciting prospect.

Sylvain
Legwinski

Personal Information

Position: Midfield
Date of Birth: 10/06/73
Weight: 73kg
Height: 186cm
Place of Birth: Clermont-Ferrand
Fee: £3.3m
Previous Clubs: Monaco, Bordeaux
Debut: Derby County (H) 25/08/01

Biography

Frenchman Sylvain Legwinski put pen to paper at Fulham in a four-year deal worth £3.3 million just after the start of the 2001/02 season. He was well known by Jean Tigana, having played under his managerial reign at Monaco. Together with John Collins, Sylvain was part of the successful Monaco side that won the French Championship in 1996/97 and reached the Semi Finals of the UEFA Cup during the same season. Sylvain joined French giants Bordeaux in January 2000, but jumped at the opportunity to work under Tigana again, this time at Fulham.

A versatile midfielder who can play in front of the back four or in a wide right position, Legwinski adds strength and depth to Fulham's midfield. Although not prolific, Leggy has the ability to set up and sometimes score vital goals at vital times. Few Fulham fans will ever forget his last minute winner at home against Tottenham during the 2002/03 season when, having gone in 2-0 down at half time, the team came back to win 3-2.

Last season fan-favourite Legwinski was once again a key cog in the Fulham midfield and deputised as Captain whenever Lee Clark was absent from the side. He signed a one year contract extension in October 2003 which will keep him at Fulham until June 2006.

Steed
Malbranque

Personal Information

Position: Midfield
Date of Birth: 06/01/80
Weight: 72kg
Height: 172cm
Place of Birth: Mouscron, Belgium
Fee: £4.5m
Previous Clubs: Lyon
Debut: Manchester Utd (A) 19/08/01

Biography

Malbranque joined Fulham from French League runners-up, Lyon, during summer 2001. He had made over 50 appearances for the French side after joining them as an 18 year-old and his six goals during his final season helped the side to win the French League Cup and to secure second place in the Championship. During the season before Steed had also played an instrumental role in earning his team a UEFA Cup Quarter Final berth.

During a hugely successful first season at Fulham, Steed carved out a reputation as a tenacious and skilful attacking midfielder who can play in a wide right position or just behind the front two. His 13 goals in 2002/03 went a long way to securing the Club's Premiership status and his purple patch mid-way through the same season saw him score in six consecutive games, including a hat-trick against Charlton in the Fourth Round of the FA Cup.

Although, by his own high standards, last season's seven goal haul was not one of his best, his contribution to the team's total of 52 League goals was immense. Playing on the right, on the left and in the middle of the park on occasion Malbranque dazzled opposing defenders and created numerous opportunities for his teammates. A sublime moment of skill on the edge of the area at home against Charlton showed the world what a magician the young Frenchman can be.

Brian
McBride

Personal Information

Position: Forward
Date of Birth: 19/06/72
Weight: 75kg
Height: 185cm
Place of Birth: Chicago, USA
Fee: Undisclosed
Previous Clubs: Columbus, Preston, Everton
Debut: Spurs (H) 31/01/04

Biography

Originally from Arlington Heights in Chicago, Illinois, 32-year-old Brian McBride arrived from Columbus Crew of the MLSin January 2004. While with Crew he was a seven-time MLS All-Star and the side's all-time leading scorer with 50 goals in 137 games.

An international star – and widely recognised as the best header of the ball in America – McBride played a starring role in the 2002 World Cup where he scored the USA's winning goals against Portugal and Mexico on route to the Quarter Finals.

He made his debut for the Whites against Tottenham last season and, within eight minutes of his second half appearance as a substitute, scored the winner in the 2-1 victory at Loftus Road. His spectacular goal against West Ham in the FA Cup Fifth Round Replay at Upton Park was also a contender for the Goal of The Season award.

Ian
Pearce

Personal Information

Position: Defence
Date of Birth: 07/05/74
Weight: 98.8kg
Height: 191cm
Place of Birth: Bury St. Edmunds
Fee: Undisclosed
Previous Clubs: Chelsea, Blackburn, West Ham
Debut: Spurs (H) 31/01/04

Biography

Central defender Ian Pearce signed in January 2004 from West Ham on a three and a half year deal that will see him at the Club until the summer of 2007.

A committed attacking central defender who can also play as a British-style centre forward, 29-year-old Pearce spent seven years at Upton Park during which time he made 135 League starts and scored nine goals. His move across London, and up a division, also saw former Fulham Club Captain Andy Melville go in the opposite direction.

Pearce began his career at Chelsea when he joined as a junior in 1991. During his two years at Stamford Bridge he made four substitute appearances for the Blues and was eventually sold for £300,000 to Blackburn in October 1993.

Pearce proved his worth at Ewood Park winning a Championship winners' medal with Rovers. In September 1997 he moved on to West Ham in a £2.3million deal and impressed hugely in the 1998/1999 season before sustaining a broken leg in the spring. Having recovered, he was then hugely unlucky to fall foul of a nasty knee ligament injury in the opening game of 1999/2000 which ruled him out for the whole season.

Since joining Fulham, Pearce has proved his Premiership credentials once again and has added strength and depth to the Fulham squad.

Mark
Pembridge

Personal Information

Position: Midfield
Date of Birth: 29/11/70
Weight: 76kg
Height: 175cm
Place of Birth: Merthyr Tydfil
Fee: Undisclosed
Previous Clubs: Luton Town, Derby County, Sheffield Wednesday, Benfica, Everton
Debut: Birmingham (A) 14/09/03

Biography

After two years at Everton 32-year-old Mark Pembridge made the move south – in the summer 2003 transfer window – to once again team up with former Wales team-mate Chris Coleman.

Pembridge signed for Everton in 1999 in a £850,000 move from Portuguese giants Benfica. However, he has studiously learned his trade from the bottom up over the years after beginning his professional career with Luton Town (70 appearances and six goals). He has also enjoyed spells at Derby County (140 appearances and 37 goals) and Sheffield Wednesday (103 appearances and 13 goals) before his move in to Europe, courtesy of Graeme Souness.

After signing for Everton, Pembridge was unlucky in that he suffered a series of niggling injuries which restricted his first team appearances in his first two seasons at the Merseyside club. But, having recovered, he enjoyed a great season last term and his combative performances for club and country earned him much respect.

However, Pembridge's first season with the Whites was somewhat dogged by injury as persistent calf problems kept him out of the side for large parts. Nevertheless, his appearances when fit proved what a committed midfielder the Welshman is and he was unlucky not to get on the scoresheet himself at Old Trafford last October

Darren
Pratley

Personal Information

Position: Midfield
Date of Birth: 22/04/85
Weight: 69.4kg
Height: 185cm
Place of Birth: Barking
Previous Clubs: Arsenal Youth
Debut: Charlton (Away) 8/11/03

Biography

Captain of the Reserve side 19-year-old Darren made his debut for the First Team in the Carling Cup game against Wigan last September and went on to make an appearance in the League game against Charlton at The Valley in November.

A central midfield player he is another Academy graduate who is surely only being kept out of the First Team by the number of central midfield players who are already established in the senior squad.

Facundo
Sava

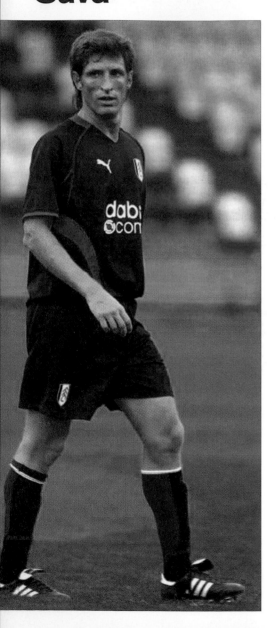

Personal Information

Position: Centre Forward
Date of Birth: 03/07/74
Weight: 83kg
Height: 183cm
Place of Birth: Argentina
Fee: £2m
Previous Clubs: Ferro, Boca Juniors, Gimnasia La Plata
Debut: FC Haka (H) 13/07/02

Biography

Fulham's first Premiership season had barely ended before the cogs in the transfer machine began to crank up once again with the arrival of Facundo Sava.

The 30 year-old Argentinian striker joined the Club in 2002 having scored 12 goals in the previous season for Argentinian Club, Gimnasia y Esgrima La Plata, as they narrowly conceded the Championship to River Plate. He also contributed to La Plata's qualification for the Libertadores Cup, South America's equivalent of the Champions League.

Sava began his career with Argentinean club Ferro before moving to the legendary Boca Juniors and then La Plata.

The mask wearing front man kept his trademark mask in his sock for much of last season but his crowd surfing moment, after scoring the winner against Bolton at Loftus Road, will live long in the memory. Played a vital role in Paul Nevin's Reserve side in 03/04.

Edwin
van der Sar

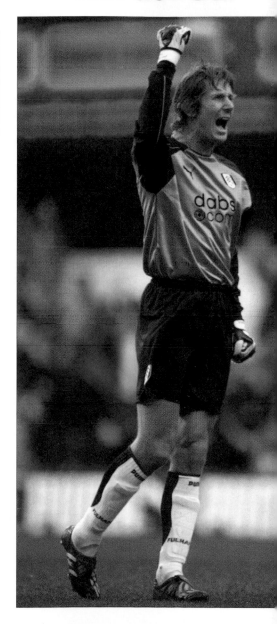

Personal Information

Position: Goalkeeper
Date of Birth: 29/10/70
Weight: 83kg
Height: 197cm
Place of Birth: Voorhout, Holland
Fee: Undisclosed
Previous Clubs: Ajax, Juventus
Debut: Manchester Utd (A) 19/08/01

Biography

Dutch International goalkeeper van der Sar joined Fulham from Italian giants Juventus on a four-year contract in summer 2001.

The 6'5" Dutchman installed himself as Juventus' number one after the departure of Angelo Peruzzi to Internazionale, becoming the first non-Italian keeper in Juve's history. However, the arrival of Gianluigi Buffon from Parma for over £30 million meant that van der Sar's opportunities in Turin became limited. Through Jean Tigana and Christian Damiano's contacts in Italy, the door to Fulham opened.

While England fans will remember van der Sar as the man who picked the ball out of his net four times in Holland's Wembley thumping during Euro '96, the Dutch know him as their most consistent performer in years. A product of the Ajax youth system and winner of the Champions League with them in 1995, he has also won the UEFA Cup, Super Cup and four Dutch League titles.

Van der Sar is incredibly agile for a big man and combines calm assurance with the ability to make outstanding saves. A deserved winner of the Player of the Season Award, van der Sar's outstanding 2003/04 campaign saw him repeatedly pulling off spectacular saves as Fulham advanced towards their highest ever League finish. A clean sheet at Highbury in the face of repeated Arsenal attacks and a penalty save at Anfield were just two highlights from a memorable year.

In summer 2004 Edwin was ever present in the Dutch side that reached the Semi Final of the European Championships and was widely touted as the keeper of the tournament.

Moritz
Volz

Personal Information

Position: Defence
Date of Birth: 21/01/83
Weight: 73.09kg
Height: 182cm
Place of Birth: Siegen, Germany
Fee: Undisclosed
Previous Clubs: Schalke 04, Arsenal,
Debut: Boro (H) 16/08/03

Biography

The departure of Steve Finnan to Liverpool in the summer of 2003 left Chris Coleman with a vital right back position to fill. Following links with a handful of players, Fulham signed Moritz Volz on loan from Arsenal until January 2004.

The German Under 20 international began his career with Shalke of the Bundesliga, but signed for the Gunners as a teenager in August 2000. With Lauren and Toure ahead of him in the Highbury pecking order, Moritz had already spent the second half of 2002/03 on loan at Wimbledon.

A pacey attacking full back, Volz impressed hugely in the first half of last season leading to a 3-year permanent deal during the January transfer window. Throughout the second half of the season, Moritz continued to impress with his attacking runs and committed defending. By the end of the campaign he had taken the statistical crown of being the most consistent tackler in the Premier League.

With the Premiership season over Volz met up with his German international team mates this summer for the Under 21 Championships in Germany.

FULHAM
FOOTBALL CLUB

www.fulhamfc.com
Follow the action all the way to the net!

Sean
Davis

Personal Information

Position: Midfield
Date of Birth: 20/09/79
Place of Birth: Lambeth
Fulham debut: Cambridge (H) 15/10/96

Biography

After retracting his transfer request in Summer 2003 Sean settled back in to the Fulham squad and scored some important goals – including his unforgettable volley against Charlton at Loftus Road.

A Fulham player in all four divisions, Sean opted to sign for Spurs in July 2004.

Jon
Harley

Personal Information

Position: Defence
Date of Birth: 26/09/79
Place of Birth: Maidstone
Debut: Manchester Utd (A) 19/08/01

Biography

With the arrival of Jerome Bonnissel last summer Jon found his chances of First Team football were limited and a loan move to West Ham in January, alongside defensive partner Andy Melville, saw him immediately claim a place in Alan Pardew's starting XI.

Scored in his first game for the Hammers and, towards the end of the season, returned to Fulham. Moved to Sheffield United this summer for whom he had previously enjoyed two successful loan spells.

Barry
Hayles

Personal Information

Position: Forward
Date of Birth: 17/04/72
Place of Birth: Lambeth
Debut: Chesterfield (H) 22/11/98

Biography

A memorable brace against Spurs at White Hart Lane was the highlight of the campaign for Barry which came after a close season operation to his neck which could have spelled the end of his career.

Barry fought his way back to full fitness and once again played an important role in a successful Fulham side. After being released by Fulham this summer Barry joined First Division Sheffield United.

Mark
Hudson

Personal Information

Position: Defence
Date of Birth: 30/03/82
Place of Birth: Guildford, Surrey
Debut: Chesterfield (A) 19/09/00

Biography

A successful loan spell at Crystal Palace propelled central defender Mark in to the limelight in the second half of the season as he helped the Eagles to the Division One Play-Offs before returning to Fulham.

Mark signed a permanent deal with Palace this summer and should be a regular in the newly promoted side.

Andy
Melville

Personal Information

Position: Defender
Date of Birth: 29/11/68
Place of Birth: Swansea
Debut: Birmingham (A) 07/08/99

Biography

Former Club Captain Andy was kept out of Chris Coleman's side for large parts of the first half of the campaign as the in-form Alain Goma and Zat Knight confined him to the bench.

Subsequently, and after five years and almost 200 First Team appearances for Fulham, he opted on a move to First Division West Ham in January. Upon joining the Upton Park outfit Andy set about establishing himself as a vital component in the team that eventually secured a place in the First Division Play-Off Final.

Bobby
Petta

Personal Information

Position: Midfielder
Date of Birth: 06/08/74
Place of Birth: Rotterdam, Netherlands
Debut: Cheltenham (A) 04/01/ 2004

Biography

A loan move from Celtic in January saw the left sided midfielder join the Whites for the second half of the campaign.

Although not a regular in the starting XI, he nevertheless proved to be a useful addition to the squad and his pace and skill added depth to the midfield.

Louis
Saha

Personal Information

Position: Striker
Date of Birth: 08/08/78
Place of Birth: Paris
Debut: Crewe (H) 12/08/00

Biography

Playing as a lone striker Fulham's top goalscorer in 2003/04 was central to Chris Coleman's side in the first half of the campaign as his 16 goals briefly rocketed the Club up to fourth in the table.

His high profile move to Manchester United in January somewhat soured his contribution but his subsequent form at Old Trafford, and selection for the France squad for Euro 2004, has merely reaffirmed his class. A true Fulham legend the importance and significance of Louis' 63 career goals for the Whites cannot be understated.

Arsenal

Useful Information

Website: www.arsenal.com
Address: Arsenal Stadium, Avenell Road, Highbury,
London N5 1BU
Main Switchboard: 020 7704 4000

Travel Information
Car Parking: Parking near the ground is difficult as
restrictions come into force.
By Train: The nearest stations are Finsbury Park
(approx 10 minutes walk) and Highbury & Islington
(approx 20 minutes walk).
By Tube: Arsenal is the nearest tube station (situated
on the Piccadilly Line).
By Bus: Numbers 4, 19 and 236 go to Blackstock
Road, the ground is approximately 10 minute walk.

Highbury

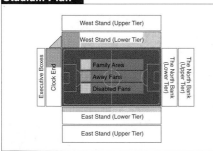

Stadium Plan

Home & Away Kit

Final Standings

Pos		W	D	L	Pts
1	Arsenal	26	12	0	90
2	**Chelsea**	**24**	**7**	**7**	**79**
3	Man Utd	23	6	9	75

All-Time Record

League matches only (home and away)

Played	Won	Drawn	Lost
34	**5**	**6**	**23**

Recent League Meetings

2003/04

Arsenal **0-0** Fulham

Fulham **0-1** Arsenal
Reyes 9

2002/03

Fulham **0-1** Arsenal
Marlet 31 (og)

Arsenal **2-1** Fulham
Pires 17, 90   Malbranque 29

2001-02

Fulham **1-3** Arsenal
Malbranque 48   Ljungberg 16
Henry 82
Bergkamp 90

Arsenal **4-1** Fulham
Lauren 5   Marlet 10
Vieira 15
Henry 39
Henry 59

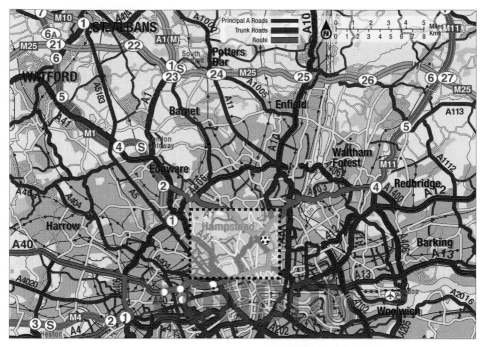

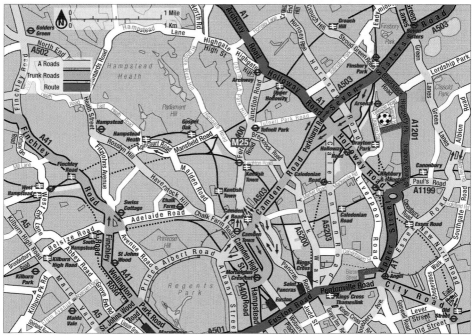

Aston Villa

Website: www.avfc.co.uk
Address: Villa Park, Trinity Road, Birmingham, B6 6HE
Main Switchboard: 0121 327 2299

Travel Information
By Train: It is a two minute walk to Villa Park from
Witton Station. Aston Station is a 10 minute walk.
Connecting trains run from Birmingham New Street.
By Bus: The number 7 runs from Birmingham City
Centre directly to the ground. Numbers 11a and 11c
also serve the ground.

Home & Away Kit

Villa Park

Stadium Plan

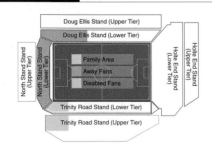

Final Standings

Pos		W	D	L	Pts
5	Newcastle	13	17	8	56
6	**Aston Villa**	**15**	**11**	**12**	**56**
7	Charlton	14	11	13	53

All-Time Record

League matches only (home and away)

Played	Won	Drawn	Lost
40	**15**	**11**	**14**

Recent League Meetings

2003/04

Aston Villa 3-0 Fulham
Angel 33
Vassell 67, 82

Fulham 1-2 Aston Villa
Boa Morte 1 | Angel 13
| Vassell 32

2002/03

Aston Villa 3-1 Fulham
Angel 20 | Boa Morte 51
Allback 66
Leonhardsen 83

Fulham 2-1 Aston Villa
Malbranque 14 (p) | Barry 3
Harley 36

2001/02

Aston Villa 2-0 Fulham
Vassell 50
Taylor 61

Fulham 0-0 Aston Villa

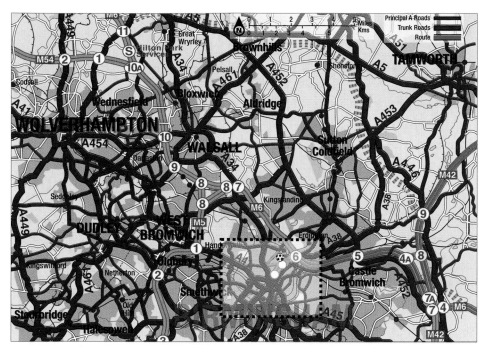

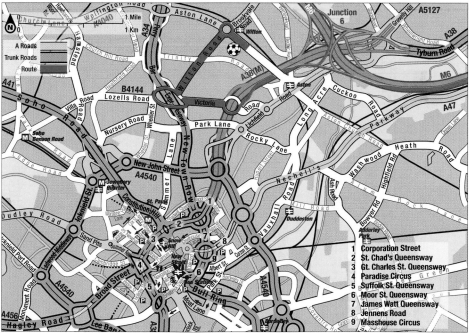

1 Corporation Street
2 St. Chad's Queensway
3 Gt. Charles St. Queensway
4 Paradise Circus
5 Suffolk St. Queensway
6 Moor St. Queensway
7 James Watt Queensway
8 Jennens Road
9 Masshouse Circus

The Opposition

Birmingham City

Useful Information

Website: www.bcfc.com
Address: St Andrew's Stadium, Birmingham B9 4NH
Main Switchboard: 0121 772 0101

Travel Information
By Train: PBirmingham New Street and Birmingham Moor Street are both roughly 20 minutes walk from the ground. Taxis from the station to the ground cost around £3.50.
By Bus: Numbers 56, 57, 57a, 58 and 60 run from the city centre to the ground. Numbers 15, 17, 96 and 97 also stop near the stadium.

St Andrew's

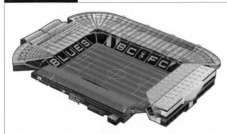

Stadium Plan

Home & Away Kit

Final Standings

Pos		W	D	L	Pts
9	Fulham	14	10	14	52
10	**Birmingham**	**12**	**14**	**12**	**50**
11	Middlesbrough	13	9	16	48

All-Time Record

League matches only (home and away)

Played	Won	Drawn	Lost
64	**19**	**21**	**24**

Recent League Meetings

2003/04
Birmingham 2-2 Fulham
Forssell 45, 82 — Saha 1
Boa Morte 78

Fulham 0-0 Birmingham

2002/03
Birmingham 0-0 Fulham

Fulham 0-1 Birmingham
Kirovski 7

2000/01 (Division One)
Birmingham 1-3 Fulham
Sonner 36 — Collins 1
Saha 31
Davis 45

Fulham 0-1 Birmingham
Grainger 49

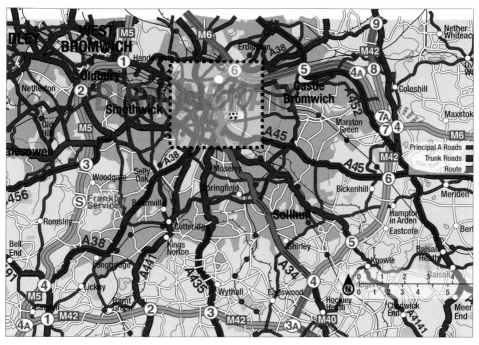

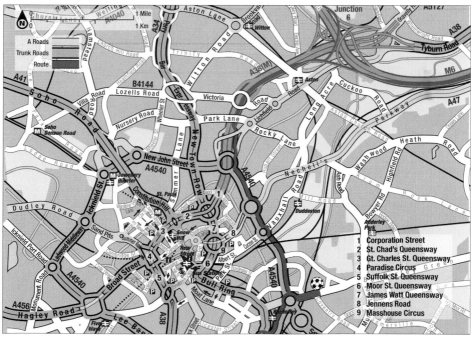

1 Corporation Street
2 St. Chad's Queensway
3 Gt. Charles St. Queensway
4 Paradise Circus
5 Suffolk St. Queensway
6 Moor St. Queensway
7 James Watt Queensway
8 Jennens Road
9 Masshouse Circus

Blackburn Rovers

Useful Information

Website: www.rovers.co.uk
Address: Ewood Park, Blackburn, Lancashire BB2 4JF
Main Switchboard: 08701 113232

Travel Information
Car Parking: Car parking can be found immediately adjacent to the stadium for up to 800 vehicles; there are three other car parks on Albion St, Albion Rd and Branch Rd on the industrial estates. Street parking is very limited.
By Train: Blackburn station is approx 11/2 miles away, Mill Hill is approx 1 mile away.
By Bus: There are 3 matchday services that run from Accrington (Route A), Intack (Route B) and Darwen (Route C). This service costs £2.00 for a return ticket. Tickets are not interchangeable between routes.

Home & Away Kit

Final Standings

Pos		W	D	L	Pts
14	Tottenham	13	6	19	45
15	**Blackburn**	**12**	**8**	**18**	**44**
16	Man City	9	14	15	41

All-Time Record

League matches only (home and away)

Played	Won	Drawn	Lost
62	**20**	**16**	**26**

Ewood Park

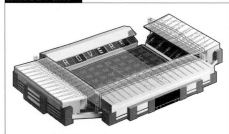

Recent League Meetings

2003/04

Blackburn 0-2 Fulham		
	Boa Morte 5	
	Saha 56	
Fulham 3-4 Blackburn		
John 26, 45	Cole 23	
Boa Morte 60	Douglas 49	
	Amoruso 51	
	Stead 75	

2002/03

Blackburn 2-1 Fulham	
Yorke 35	Marlet 60
Fulham 0-4 Blackburn	
	Dunn 37 (p)
	Sukur 42
	Duff 53
	Sukur 54

2001/02

Fulham 2-0 Blackburn	
Hayles 31	
Malbranque 63	
Blackburn 3-0 Fulham	
Cole 52, 82	
Duff 66	

Stadium Plan

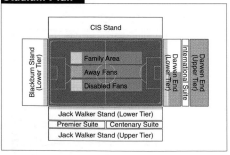

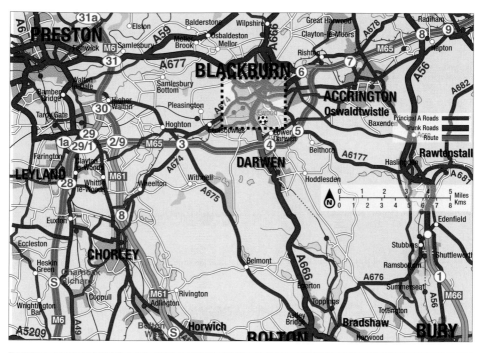

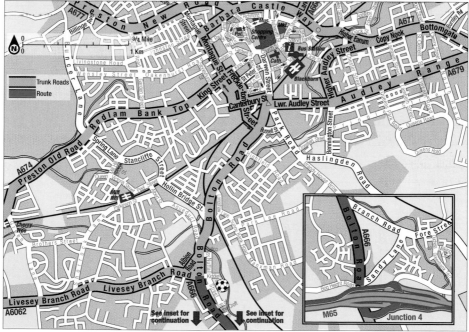

Bolton Wanderers

Useful Information

Website: www.bwfc.co.uk
Address: The Reebok Stadium, Burnden Way,
Bolton BL6 6JW
Main Switchboard: 01204 673 673

Travel Information
Car Parking: Parking is available in the allocated away
parking area for £5. Follow signs for car park 'A'. There
is also some parking available at British Aerospace for
£3, some of which goes to charity. This is past
the signs for car park 'A' and right at the next
set of traffic lights.
By Train: Horwich Parkway station is a two minute
walk from the ground. Bolton station is approx 5 miles
away from the Reebok stadium.
By Bus: The club runs buses from Bolton town centre
to the ground for £1.30 return. In addition,
the number 539 bus runs directly to the ground.

Reebok Stadium

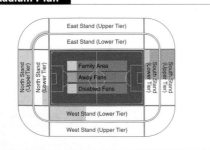

Stadium Plan

Home & Away Kit

Final Standings

Pos		W	D	L	Pts
7	Charlton	14	11	13	53
8	**Bolton**	**14**	**11**	**13**	**53**
9	Fulham	14	10	14	52

All-Time Record

League matches only (home and away)

Played	Won	Drawn	Lost
60	**20**	**16**	**24**

Recent League Meetings

2003/04

Fulham 2-1 Bolton
S.Davis 75   Davies 53
Sava 76

Bolton 0-2 Fulham
McBride 45, 78

2002/03

Fulham 4-1 Bolton
Saha (p) 11   Ricketts 4 (p)
Legwinski 33
Marlet (p) 38
Legwinski 79

Bolton 0-0 Fulham

2001/02

Bolton 0-0 Fulham

Fulham 3-0 Bolton
Goldbaek 42
Marlet 72
Hayles 76

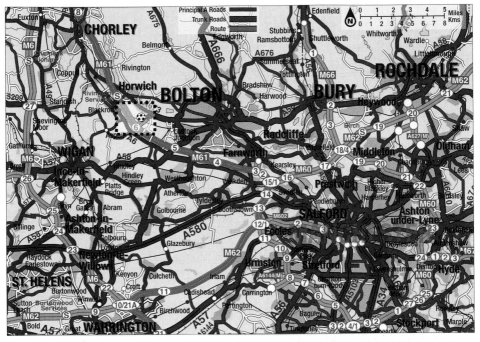

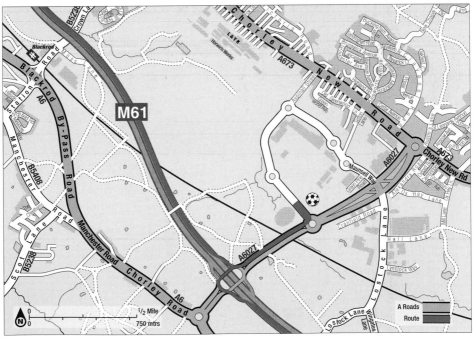

Charlton Athletic

Useful Information

Website: www.cafc.co.uk
Address: The Valley, Floyd Road, Charlton, London SE7 8BL
Main Switchboard: 020 8333 4000

Travel Information
Car Parking: Parking is available on Victoria Way, an 8 minute walk from the ground. It costs £5 and payment is on the gate. Street parking is very limited around the ground and public transport is recommended.
By Train: Trains run from Charing Cross, London Bridge and Waterloo East to Charlton station, approx. 2 minutes walk. Turn right out of station and the left into Floyd Road. North Greenwich on the Jubilee Line has bus links to the ground.
By Bus: Numbers 177 (towards Peckham), 180 (towards Lewisham), 53 (towards Plumstead) or 54 (toward Woolwich). 161, 422, 472, 486 (towards North Greenwich).

Home & Away Kit

The Valley

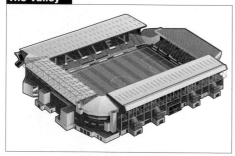

Stadium Plan

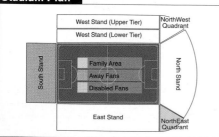

Final Standings

Pos		W	D	L	Pts
6	Aston Villa	15	11	12	56
7	**Charlton**	**14**	**11**	**13**	**53**
8	Bolton	14	11	13	53

All-Time Record

League matches only (home and away)

Played	Won	Drawn	Lost
48	**17**	**15**	**16**

Recent League Meetings

2003/04

Charlton 3-1 Fulham
Stuart 10   S.Davis 89
Johansson 69, 76

Fulham 2-0 Charlton
Malbranque 18 (p)
S.Davis 64

2002/03

Fulham 1-0 Charlton
Sava 36

Charlton 0-1 Fulham
Saha 33 (p)

2001/02

Charlton 1-1 Fulham
Melville (og) 34

Fulham 0-0 Charlton

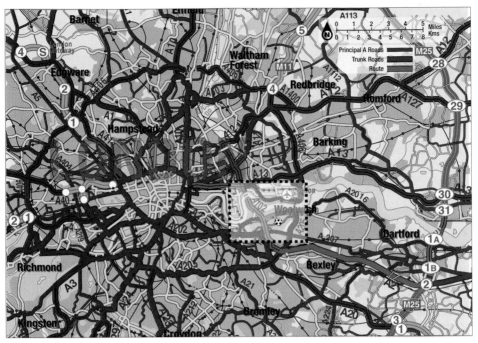

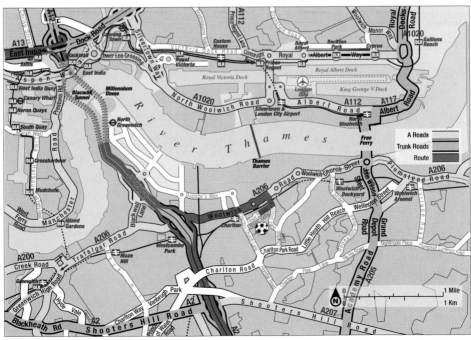

Chelsea

Website: www.chelseafc.com
Address: Stamford Bridge, Fulham Road,
London SW6 1HS
Main Switchboard: 020 7385 5545

Travel Information
Car Parking: Parking restrictions during
the game make it advisable to travel by tube. Limited
on-site matchday underground parking is available in
advance: 0207 915 1956
By Tube: Fulham Broadway is on the District Line,
approx 5 minutes walk. Turn left out of station and
ground is on the left hand side.
By Bus: Numbers 14 (towards Tottenham Court
Road), 414 and 211 (towards Hammersmith) go
along Fulham Road. Numbers 11, 14, 28, 211, 295,
391, 414, 424 all stop near the ground.

Stamford Bridge

Stadium Plan

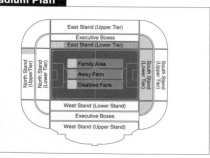

Home & Away Kit

Final Standings

Pos		W	D	L	Pts
1	Arsenal	26	12	0	90
2	**Chelsea**	**24**	**7**	**7**	**79**
3	Man Utd	23	6	9	75

All-Time Record

League matches only (home and away)

Played	Won	Drawn	Lost
50	**6**	**15**	**29**

Recent League Meetings

2003/04

Fulham 0-1 Chelsea
　　　　　　　　Crespo 62

Chelsea 2-1 Fulham
Gudjohnsen 7　　Pembridge 19
Duff 30

2002/03

Fulham 0-0 Chelsea

Chelsea 1-1 Fulham
Goma (og) 39　　Boa Morte 66

2001/02

Fulham 1-1 Chelsea
Hayles 55　　Hasselbaink 32

Chelsea 3-2 Fulham
Melchiot 17　　Saha 19 (p), 73
Gudjohnsen 28
Forssell 83

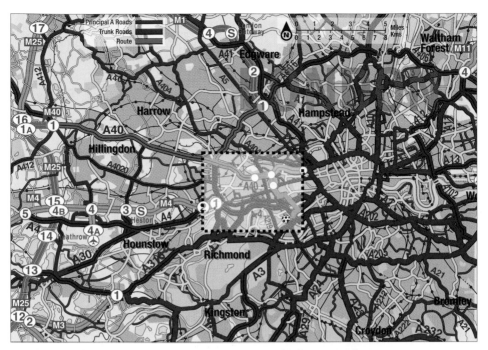

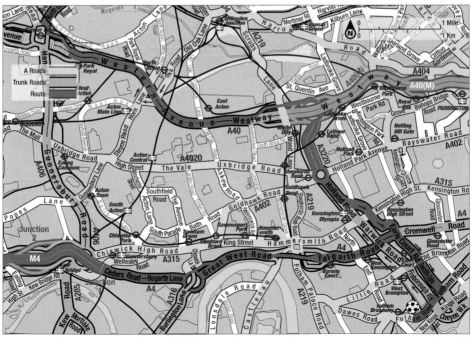

The Opposition

Crystal Palace

Useful Information

Website: www.cpfc.co.uk
Address: Selhurst Park, South Norwood,
London SE25 6PU
Main Switchboard: 020 8768 6000

Travel Information
Car Parking: There are limited car parking at the
ground. The best area is Sellurst station. The roads
in Thornton Heath are mostly pay-and-display.
By Train: Thornton Heath, Selhurst and Norwood
Junction stations are all a five-minute walk from the
ground. Trains run from Victoria or London Bridge.
By Bus: Numbers 468, 196 and 410.

Home & Away Kit

Selhurst Park

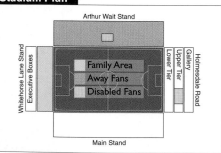

Stadium Plan

Final Standings

Pos		W	D	L	Pts
5	Ipswich	21	10	15	73
6	**Crystal Palace**	**21**	**10**	**15**	**73**
7	Wigan	18	17	11	71

All-Time Record

League matches only (home and away)

Played	Won	Drawn	Lost
36	**14**	**13**	**9**

Recent League Meetings

2000/01 (Division One)

Crystal Palace 0-2 Fulham
Boa Morte 15, 69

Fulham 3-1 Crystal Palace
Saha 10   Ruddock 17
Clark 23, 59

1999/2000 (Division One)

Fulham 1-0 Crystal Palace
Horsfield 17

Crystal Palace 0-0 Fulham

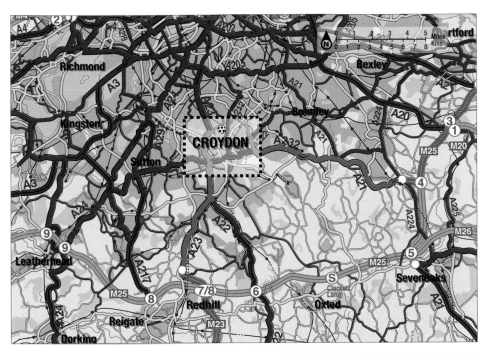

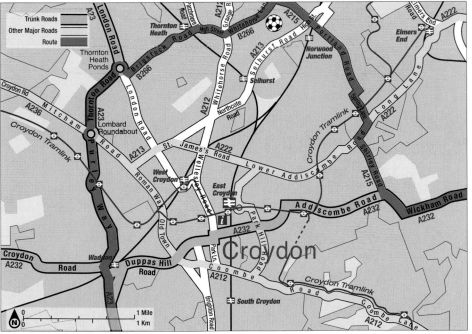

Everton

Useful Information

Website: www.evertonfc.com
Address: Goodison Park, Liverpool L4 4EL
Main Switchboard: 0151 330 2200

Travel Information
Car Parking: 1000 spaces are available at Stanley
Park, costing £6. Street parking is residents only
By Train: Take any train from Liverpool Central which is
heading for Ormskirk or Kirkby and alight at Kirkdale,
a 10 minute walk from the ground.
By Bus: The number 19 runs from the Queen's Square
bus station to Walton Lane; the number 20 runs along
Spellow Lane.

Goodison Park

Stadium Plan

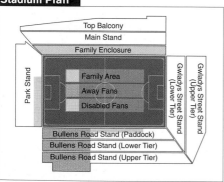

Home & Away Kit

Final Standings

Pos		W	D	L	Pts
16	Man City	9	14	15	41
17	**Everton**	**9**	**12**	**17**	**39**
18	Leicester	6	15	17	33

All-Time Record

League matches only (home and away)

Played	Won	Drawn	Lost
32	**9**	**8**	**15**

Recent League Meetings

2003/04

Everton 3-1 Fulham
Naysmith 7   Hayles 69
Unsworth 20
Watson 35

Fulham 2-1 Everton
Saha 45 (p)   Kilbane 81
Malbranque 46

2002/03

Everton 2-0 Fulham
Gravesen 45
Campbell 45

Fulham 2-0 Everton
Stubbs 34 (og)
Wright 43 (og)

2001/02

Fulham 2-0 Everton
Hayles 36, 50

Everton 2-1 Fulham
Unsworth 1   Malbranque 52
Ferguson 12

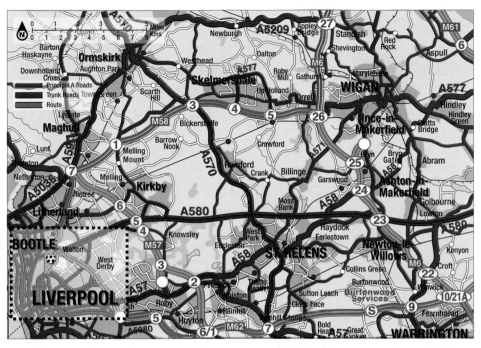

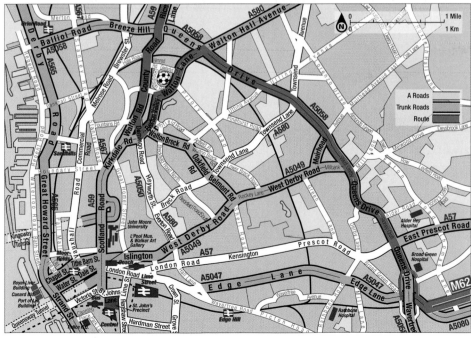

Liverpool

Useful Information

Website: www.liverpoolfc.tv
Address: Anfield Road, Liverpool L4 0TH
Main Switchboard: 0151 263 2361

Travel Information
By Train: Lime Street Railway Station is in the town centre, 2 miles from Anfield. Kirkdale Railway Station is 30 minutes walk from the ground. Frequent Soccerbus shuttles run from Sandhills Station two hours before each match and 50 minutes after the final whistle.
By Bus: Numbers 26 and 27 run from Paradise Street bus station. Numbers 5, 17b, 17c, 17d and 217 run from Queen Square bus station. There is a 'Soccerbus' service that runs from Sandhills station to Anfield for two hours before the match and 50 minutes afterwards.

Anfield

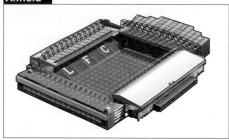

Stadium Plan

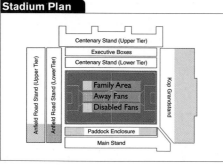

Home & Away Kit

Final Standings

Pos		W	D	L	Pts
3	Man Utd	23	6	9	75
4	**Liverpool**	**16**	**12**	**10**	**60**
5	Newcastle	13	17	8	56

All-Time Record

League matches only (home and away)

Played	Won	Drawn	Lost
34	**5**	**11**	**18**

Recent League Meetings

2003/04

Fulham 1-2 Liverpool
Saha 40   Heskey 17
Murphy 89 (p)

Liverpool 0-0 Fulham

2002/03

Fulham 3-2 Liverpool
Sava 5, 68   Hamann 62
Davis 38   Baros 86

Liverpool 2-0 Fulham
Heskey 36
Owen 59

2001/02

Liverpool 0-0 Fulham

Fulham 0-2 Liverpool
Anelka 13
Litmanen 90

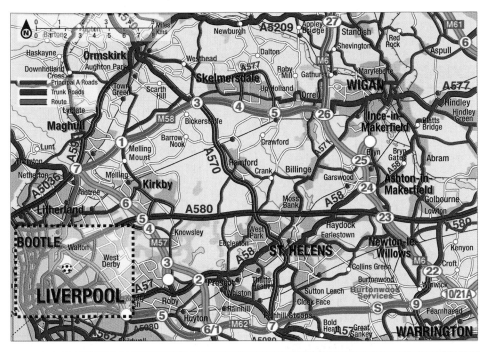

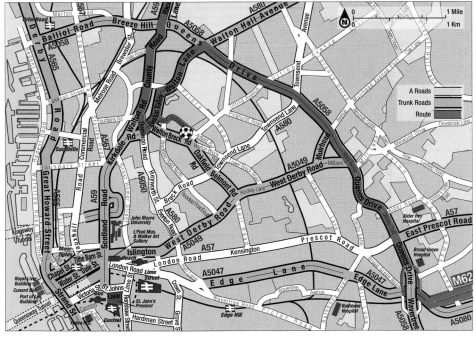

Manchester City

Useful Information

Website: www.mcfc.co.uk
Address: City of Manchester Stadium, Sportcity,
Manchester M11 3FF
Main Switchboard: 0161 231 3200

Travel Information
By Train: The nearest station is Manchester Picadilly,
approx 1 mile from the stadium
By Bus: Numbers 216, 217, and 230 to 237 run
from the city centre

Home & Away Kit

The City of Manchester Stadium

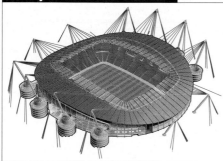

Stadium Plan

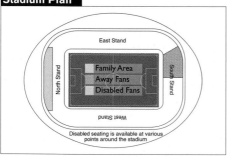

Final Standings

Pos		W	D	L	Pts
15	Blackburn	12	8	18	44
16	**Man City**	**9**	**14**	**15**	**41**
17	Everton	9	12	17	39

All-Time Record

League matches only (home and away)

Played	Won	Drawn	Lost
38	**11**	**8**	**19**

Recent League Meetings

2003/04

Fulham 2-2 Man City

Malbranque 73	Knight 46 (og)
Saha 79	Wanchope 90

Man City 0-0 Fulham

2002/03

Fulham 0-1 Man City

Anelka 84

Man City 4-1 Fulham

Anelka 21	Malbranque 2
Benarbia 47	
Foe 61	
Wright-Phillips 70	

1999/2000 (Division One)
Fulham 0-0 Man City

Man City 4-0 Fulham
Goater 29, 77, 85
Horlock 87 (p)

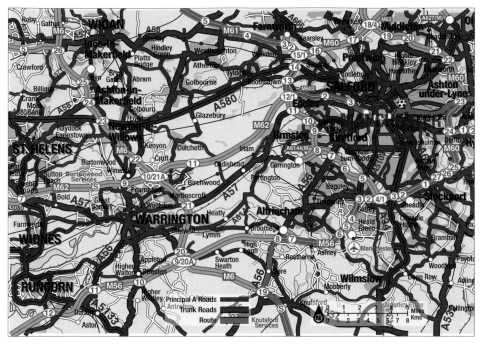

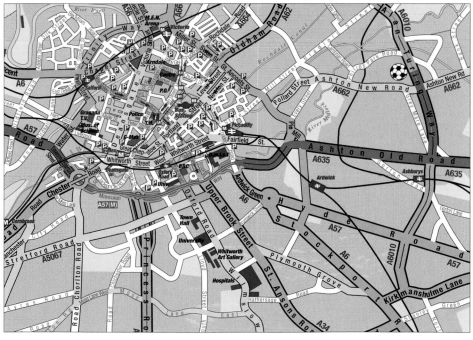

Manchester Utd

Useful Information

Website: www.manutd.com
Address: Sir Matt Busby Way, Old Trafford,
Manchester M16 ORA
Main Switchboard: 0161 868 8000

Travel Information
Car Parking: There is a large official car park on
Elevator Road, and various smaller car parks nearby.
By Metrolink: Old Trafford station is about 1/2 mile
away from the ground.
By Train: (matchdays only): Special services run from the
clubs own railway station adjacent to the south stand.
By Bus: Numbers 114, 230, 252 and 253 all run from
the city centre to the ground.

Home & Away Kit

Final Standings

Pos		W	D	L	Pts
2	Chelsea	24	7	7	79
3	**Man Utd**	**23**	**6**	**9**	**75**
4	Liverpool	16	12	10	60

Old Trafford

All-Time Record

League matches only (home and away)

Played	Won	Drawn	Lost
48	**10**	**12**	**26**

Recent League Meetings

2003/04

Man Utd 1-3 Fulham
Forlan 45 — Clark 3
Malbranque 66
Inamoto 76

Fulham 1-1 Man Utd
Boa Morte 64 — Saha 14

2002/03

Fulham 1-1 Man Utd
Marlet 35 — Solskjaer 62
Man Utd 3-0 Fulham
van Nistelrooy 45 (p), 68, 90

2001/02

Man Utd 3-2 Fulham
Beckham 35 — Saha 4, 48
van Nistelrooy 51, 53

Fulham 2-3 Man Utd
Legwinski 45 — Giggs 5, 47
Marlet 89 — van Nistelrooy 45

Stadium Plan

North Stand (Tier 3)
Executive Boxes
North Stand (Upper Tier)
Executive Boxes
North Stand (Lower Tier)
West Stand (Upper Tier)
Executive Boxes
West Stand (Lower Tier)
Family Area
Away Fans
Disabled Fans
East Stand (Lower Tier)
Executive Boxes
East Stand (Upper Tier)
South Stand
Executive Boxes

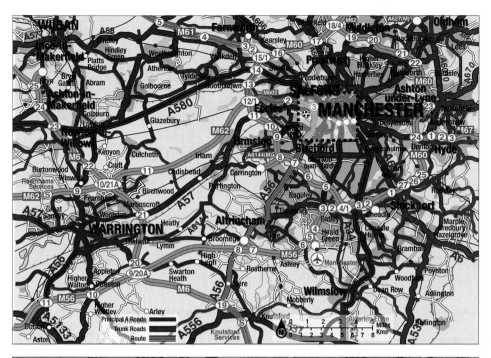

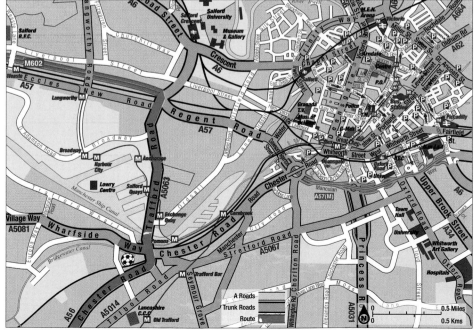

Middlesbrough

Useful Information

Website: www.mfc.co.uk
Address: Riverside Stadium, Middlesbrough,
Cleveland TS3 6RS
Main Switchboard: 01642 877700

Travel Information
Car Parking: There are various multi-storey car parks
in the town centre, which fans are encouraged to use
and walk to the ground, approx 15 minutes away.
By Train: Middlesbrough station is about 15 minutes
walk from the ground, take the back exit from the
station, turn right, then after a couple of minutes right
again into Windward Way.
By Bus: The numbers 36, 37 and 38 go from the
town centre to within a short walking distance of
the ground.

The Riverside Stadium

Stadium Plan

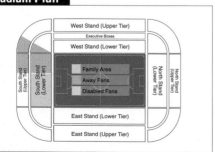

Home & Away Kit

Final Standings

Pos		W	D	L	Pts
10	Birmingham	12	14	12	50
11	**Middlesbrough**	**13**	**9**	**16**	**48**
12	Southampton	12	11	15	47

All-Time Record

League matches only (home and away)

Played	Won	Drawn	Lost
46	**19**	**6**	**21**

Recent League Meetings

2003/04

Fulham	**3-2**	**Middlesbrough**
Marlet 18		Marinelli 10
Inamoto 56		Nemeth 81
Saha 70		

Middlesbrough	**2-1**	**Fulham**
Job 15		Hayles 90
Nemeth 67		

2002/03

Middlesbrough	**2-2**	**Fulham**
Maccarone 32, 51		Sava 90
		Davis 90

Fulham	**1-0**	**Middlesbrough**
Davis 39		

2001/02

Fulham	**2-1**	**Middlesbrough**
Saha 40		Cooper 8
Marlet 45		

Middlesbrough	**2-1**	**Fulham**
Boksic 26		Marlet 56
Nemeth 78		

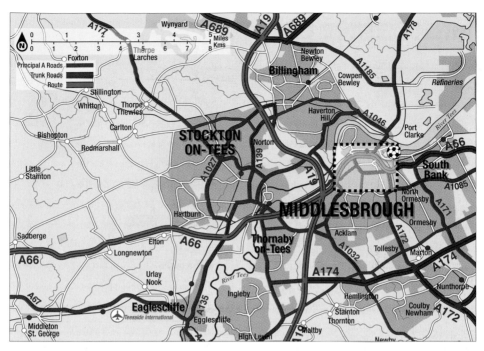

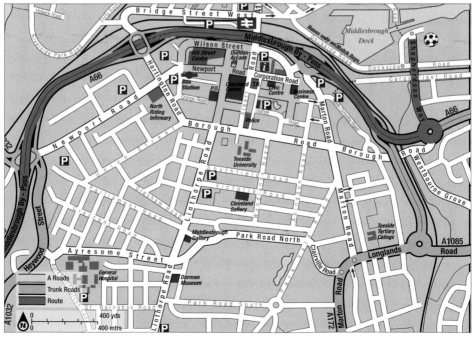

Newcastle United

Useful Information

Website: www.nufc.co.uk
Address: St James' Park,
Newcastle-upon-Tyne NE1 4ST
Main Switchboard: 0191 201 8400

Travel Information
Car Parking: There is no parking within the confines of
St. James' Park. However there are extensive parking
facilities in the City Centre which is a very short walk
to the stadium.
By Train: St James' Park is a short 5-minute walk from
the British Rail Central Station. Turn left out of the
station onto Neville Street, past two sets of lights and
right into St James' Boulevard. You will be able to see
St. James' Park ahead of you at the top of St. James'
Boulevard. The stadium is also served by its own
Metro station adjacent to the ground (St James Metro).
By Bus: Catch a bus from the town centre heading
towards Gallowgate.

St James' Park

Stadium Plan

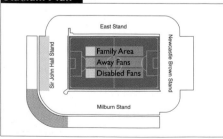

Home & Away Kit

Final Standings

Pos		W	D	L	Pts
4	Liverpool	16	12	10	60
5	**Newcastle**	**13**	**17**	**8**	**56**
6	Aston Villa	15	11	12	56

All-Time Record

League matches only (home and away)

Played	Won	Drawn	Lost
44	**17**	**11**	**16**

Recent League Meetings

2003/04

Fulham	**2-3**	**Newcastle**
Clark 5		Robert 15
Saha 7		Shearer 50 (p), 55

Newcastle	**3-1**	**Fulham**
O'Brien 4		Davis 74
Speed 41		
Robert 54		

2002/03

Newcastle	**2-0**	**Fulham**
Solano 8		
Bellamy 70		

Fulham	**2-1**	**Newcastle**
Legwinski 69		Shearer 39
Clark 86		

2001/02

Fulham	**3-1**	**Newcastle**
Saha 20		Speed 66
Legwinski 28		
Hayles 70		

Newcastle	**1-1**	**Fulham**
Dyer 21		Saha 76

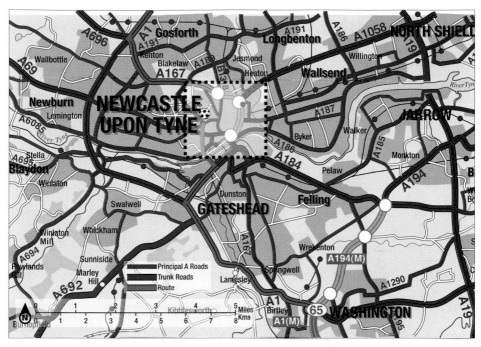

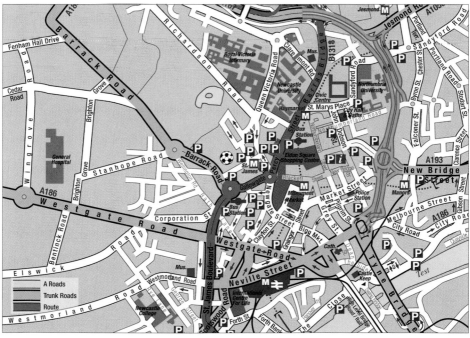

Norwich City

Useful Information

Website: www.canaries.co.uk
Address: Carrow Road, Norwich NR1 1JE
Main Switchboard: 01603 760 760

Travel Information
There are designated car parks in the surrounding area. Norwich station in within walking distance (approx 10 minutes) of Carrow Road.

Home & Away Kit

Carrow Road

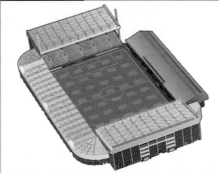

Stadium Plan

Final Standings

Pos		W	D	L	Pts
1	Norwich	28	10	8	94
2	**West Brom**	**25**	**11**	**10**	**86**
3	Sunderland	22	13	11	79

All-Time Record

League matches only (home and away)

Played	Won	Drawn	Lost
30	**11**	**9**	**10**

Recent League Meetings

2000/01 (Division One)

Fulham 2-0 Norwich
Saha 39
Boa Morte 90

Norwich 0-1 Fulham
Boa Morte 88

1999/2000 (Division One)

Fulham 1-1 Norwich
Symons 9   Roberts 53

Norwich 1-2 Fulham
Forbes 29   Riedle 73
Hayles 88

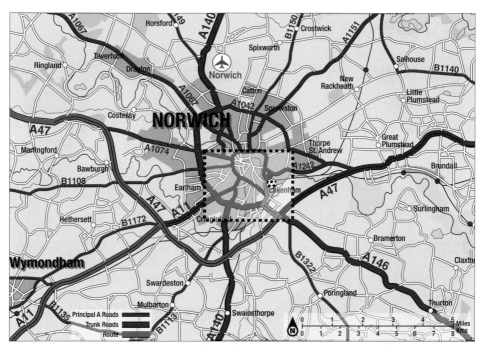

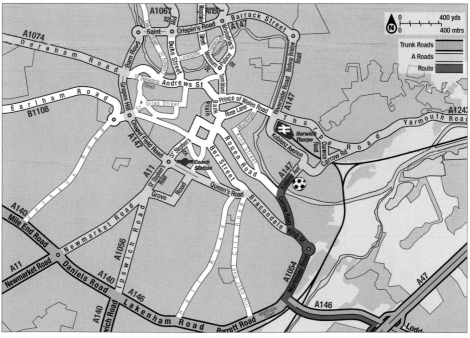

Portsmouth

Useful Information

Website: www.pompeyfc.co.uk
Address: Fratton Park, Frogmore Road,
Portsmouth PO4 8RA
Main Switchboard: 023 9273 1204

Travel Information
By Train: Fratton station is a short walk from the ground.
By Bus: Numbers 3, 13, 14, 16a, 24, 27 and 57 all run
to Fratton station.

Home & Away Kit

Fratton Park

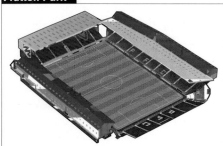

Stadium Plan

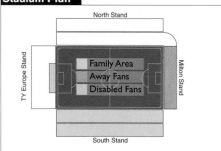

Final Standings

Pos		W	D	L	Pts
12	Southampton	12	11	15	47
13	**Portsmouth**	**12**	**9**	**17**	**45**
14	Tottenham	13	6	19	45

All-Time Record

League matches only (home and away)

Played	Won	Drawn	Lost
40	**9**	**14**	**17**

Recent League Meetings

2003/04

Fulham 2-0 Portsmouth
Saha 30, 33

Portsmouth 1-1 Fulham
Ayegbeni 80 · McBride 85

2000/01 (Division One)
Portsmouth 1-1 Fulham
Bradbury 10 · Saha 79 (p)

Fulham 3-1 Portsmouth
Hayles 11, 69 · Claridge 44
Clark 80

1999/2000 (Division One)
Portsmouth 0-1 Fulham
Goldbaek 71

Fulham 1-0 Portsmouth
Collins 89

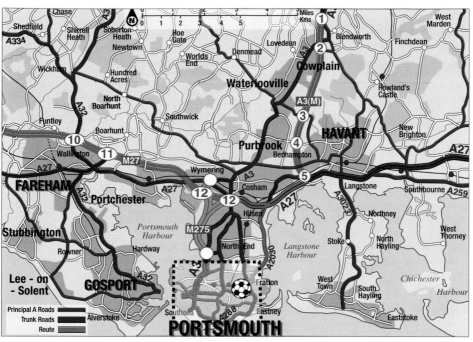

Principal A Roads
Trunk Roads
Route

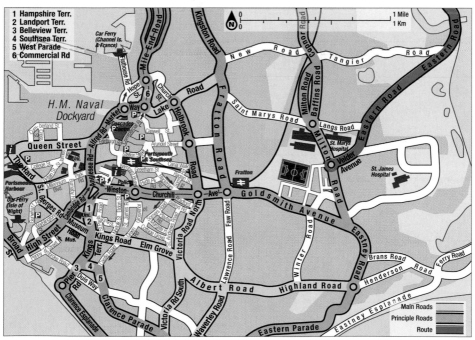

1 Hampshire Terr.
2 Landport Terr.
3 Belleview Terr.
4 Southsea Terr.
5 West Parade
6 Commercial Rd

Main Roads
Principle Roads
Route

Southampton

Useful Information

Website: www.saintsfc.co.uk
Address: The Friends Provident St Mary's Stadium, Britannia Road, Southampton, Hants SO14 5FP
Main Switchboard: 0870 220 0000

Travel Information
Car Parking: The club urge people not to head towards the stadium by car as the surrounding area is subject to police restrictions. Parking for both home and visiting supporters maybe available, but bookings must be made in advance. Please phone 0870 220 0150 for details.
By Train/Bus: The nearest station to the ground is Southampton Central. Shuttle buses run from the station to the stadium two hours before the game up until kick off.

The Friends Provident

Stadium Plan

Home & Away Kit

Final Standings

Pos		W	D	L	Pts
11	Middlesbrough	13	9	16	48
12	**Southampton**	**12**	**11**	**15**	**47**
13	Portsmouth	12	9	17	45

All-Time Record

League matches only (home and away)

Played	Won	Drawn	Lost
52	**15**	**16**	**21**

Recent League Meetings

2003/04

Fulham 2-0 Southampton
Saha 19
Saha 63 (p)

Southampton 0-0 Fulham

2002/03

Southampton 4-2 Fulham
Beattie 27 (p), 42, 53   Clark 15
Ormerod 72   Malbranque 25

Fulham 2-2 Southampton
Saha 44   Beattie 81
M.Svensson 52 (og)   M.Svensson 90

2001/02

Fulham 2-1 Southampton
Malbranque 24, 32   Beattie 32
Southampton 1-1 Fulham
Delap 21   Marlet 7

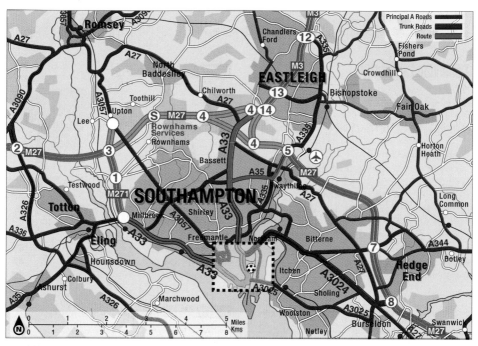

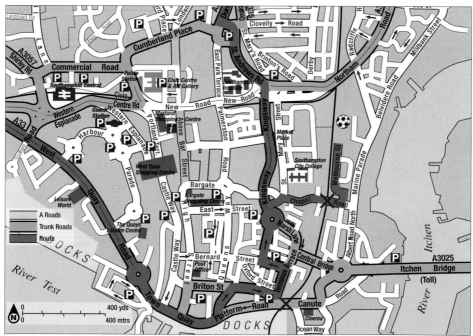

Tottenham Hotspur

Useful Information

Website: www.spurs.co.uk
Address: Bill Nicholson Way, 748 High Road,
Tottenham, London N17 0AP
Main Switchboard: 020 8365 5000

Travel Information
Car Parking: Limited parking is available near
the ground.
By Train/Tube: The nearest Underground station is
Seven Sisters (Victoria Line), approx 30 minute
walk. The nearest station is White Hart Lane, approx
5 minutes walk, on the Liverpool Street-Enfield
Town line.
By Bus: Numbers 149, 259 and 279 all go along
Tottenham High Road.

Home & Away Kit

White Hart Lane

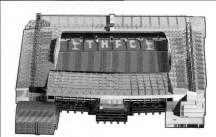

Stadium Plan

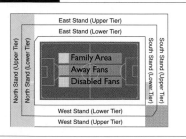

Final Standings

Pos		W	D	L	Pts
13	Portsmouth	12	9	17	45
14	**Tottenham**	**13**	**6**	**19**	**45**
15	Blackburn	12	8	18	44

All-Time Record

League matches only (home and away)

Played	Won	Drawn	Lost
50	**7**	**19**	**24**

Recent League Meetings

2003/04

Tottenham 0-3 Fulham	
	Hayles 23, 62
	Boa Morte 71
Fulham 2-1 Tottenham	
Malbranque 45 (p)	Keane 18 (p)
McBride 67	

2002/03

Fulham 3-2 Tottenham	
Inamoto 68	Richards 36
Malbranque 84 (p)	Sheringham 44
Legwinski 90	
Tottenham 1-1 Fulham	
Sheringham 40 (p)	King 15 (og)

2001/02

Tottenham 4-0 Fulham	
Ferdinand 20	
Anderton 40	
Davies 71	
Rebrov 77	
Fulham 0-2 Tottenham	
	Sheringham 28
	Poyet 31

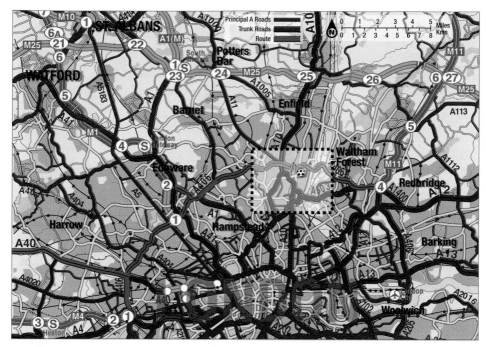

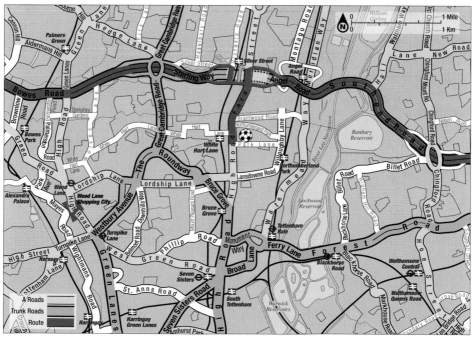

West Bromwich Albion

Useful Information

Website: www.wba.co.uk
Address: The Hawthorns, Halfords Lane,
West Bromwich, West Midlands B71 4LF
Main Switchboard: 0121 525 8888

Travel Information
Car Parking: There is limited parking available in the
East Stand car park and the surrounding streets.
By Train: Trains run to Hawthorns station from Snow
Hill, which is a five minute walk from New Street
station, Birmingham.

The Hawthorns

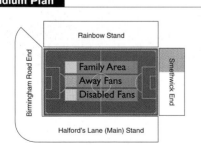

Stadium Plan

Home & Away Kit

Final Standings

Pos		W	D	L	Pts
1	Norwich	28	10	8	94
2	**West Brom**	**25**	**11**	**10**	**86**
3	Sunderland	22	13	11	79

All-Time Record

League matches only (home and away)

Played	Won	Drawn	Lost
58	**18**	**11**	**29**

Recent League Meetings

2002/03

West Brom 1-0 Fulham
Moore 48

Fulham 3-0 West Brom
Saha 72
Wome 74
Malbranque 77 (p)

2000/01 (Division One)
West Brom 1-3 Fulham
Lyttle 72   Davis 4, 28
Stolcers 87
Fulham 0-0 West Brom

1999/2000 (Division One)
West Brom 0-0 Fulham

Fulham 1-0 West Brom
Riedle 48 (p)

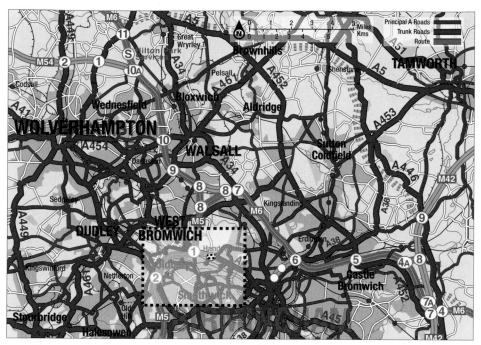

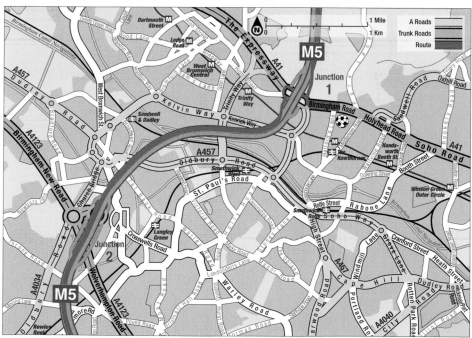

Home fixture

In this fixture...

Date	Opposition	03-04 scoreline	Played	Premiership history	Goals for	Goals against	⚽	►	W	D	L	Most common score (no. times)	Avg time of first goal (mins)	Avg no. of corners
14th Aug	Man City	0 - 0	2	----------LD	1	4	1	►	0	0	1	4-1 (1x)	2	2
21st Aug	Bolton	2 - 1	3	--------WWW	9	2	1	►	1	0	0	4-1 (1x)	43	5
25th Aug	Middlesbro	3 - 2	3	--------WWW	6	3	1	►	1	0	0	3-2 (1x)	32	7
30th Aug	Portsmouth	1 - 1	1	----------D	1	1	0	►	0	0	0	1-1 (1x)	85	3
11th Sep	Arsenal	0 - 1	3	--------LLL	1	5	0	►	0	0	0	0-1 (2x)	48	6
18th Sep	West Brom	n/a	1	----------L-	0	1	0	►	0	0	0	1-0 (1x)	N/A	7
25th Sep	Southampton	2 - 0	3	--------WDW	6	3	3	►	2	1	0	2-2 (1x)	29	7
4th Oct	C Palace	n/a	These teams have never played each other in the Premiership											
16th Oct	Liverpool	1 - 2	3	--------LWL	4	6	1	►	1	0	0	3-2 (1x)	23	5
23rd Oct	Aston Villa	0 - 3	3	--------LLL	1	8	0	►	0	0	0	3-1 (1x)	51	4
30th Oct	Tottenham	2 - 1	3	--------LWW	5	5	0	►	0	0	0	3-2 (1x)	57	8
6th Nov	Newcastle	1 - 3	3	--------DLL	2	6	0	►	0	0	0	3-1 (1x)	75	4
13th Nov	Chelsea	0 - 1	3	--------DDL	1	2	0	►	0	0	0	1-1 (1x)	55	4
20th Nov	Everton	1 - 3	3	--------LLL	2	7	0	►	0	0	0	3-1 (1x)	61	8
27th Nov	Blackburn	3 - 4	3	--------WLL	5	8	1	►	1	0	0	3-4 (1x)	29	4
4th Dec	Norwich	n/a	These teams have never played each other in the Premiership											
13th Dec	Man Utd	1 - 1	3	--------LDD	4	5	1	►	0	1	0	1-1 (2x)	48	4
20th Dec	Charlton	1 - 3	3	--------DWL	3	4	1	►	1	0	0	3-1 (1x)	53	5
26th Dec	Arsenal	0 - 0	3	--------LLD	2	6	0	►	0	0	0	4-1 (1x)	20	3

Home fixture

In this fixture...

Date	Opposition	03-04 scoreline	Played	Premiership history	Goals for	Goals against	No. of times Fulham scored first and the result that followed		W	D	L	Most common score (no. times)	Avg time of first goal (mins)	Avg no. of corners	Home
28th Dec	Birmingham	0 - 0	2	----------LD	0	1	0	►	0	0	0	0-1 (1x)	N/A	4	🏠
1st Jan	C Palace	n/a		These teams have never played each other in the Premiership											🏠
3rd Jan	Southampton	0 - 0	3	---------DLD	3	5	2	►	0	1	1	4-2 (1x)	11	5	
15th Jan	West Brom	n/a	1	---------W-	3	0	1	►	1	0	0	3-0 (1x)	72	2	🏠
22nd Jan	Birmingham	2 - 2	2	---------DD	2	2	1	►	0	1	0	2-2 (1x)	1	2	
2nd Feb	Aston Villa	1 - 2	3	---------DWL	3	3	1	►	0	0	1	2-1 (1x)	8	7	🏠
5th Feb	Liverpool	0 - 0	3	---------DLD	0	2	0	►	0	0	0	0-0 (2x)	N/A	5	
12th Feb	Newcastle	2 - 3	3	---------WWL	7	5	2	►	1	0	1	3-1 (1x)	31	4	🏠
26th Feb	Tottenham	3 - 0	3	---------LDW	4	5	2	►	1	1	0	4-0 (1x)	19	5	
5th Mar	Charlton	2 - 0	3	---------DWW	3	0	2	►	2	0	0	2-0 (1x)	27	4	🏠
19th Mar	Man Utd	3 - 1	3	---------LLW	5	7	2	►	1	0	1	3-2 (1x)	4	4	
2nd Apr	Portsmouth	2 - 0	1	----------W	2	0	1	►	1	0	0	2-0 (1x)	30	2	🏠
9th Apr	Bolton	2 - 0	3	---------DDW	2	0	1	►	1	0	0	0-0 (2x)	45	3	
16th Apr	Man City	2 - 2	2	---------LD	2	3	0	►	0	0	0	2-2 (1x)	73	3	🏠
19th Apr	Middlesbro	1 - 2	3	---------LDL	4	6	0	►	0	0	0	2-1 (2x)	79	8	
23rd Apr	Chelsea	1 - 2	3	---------LDL	4	6	0	►	0	0	0	3-2 (1x)	35	3	
30th Apr	Everton	2 - 1	3	---------WWW	6	1	3	►	3	0	0	2-0 (2x)	38	6	🏠
7th May	Blackburn	2 - 0	3	---------LLW	3	5	1	►	1	0	0	3-0 (1x)	33	5	
14th May	Norwich	n/a		These teams have never played each other in the Premiership											🏠